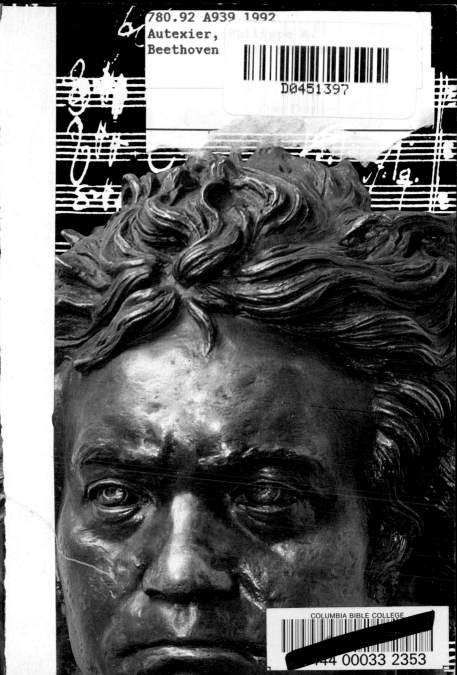

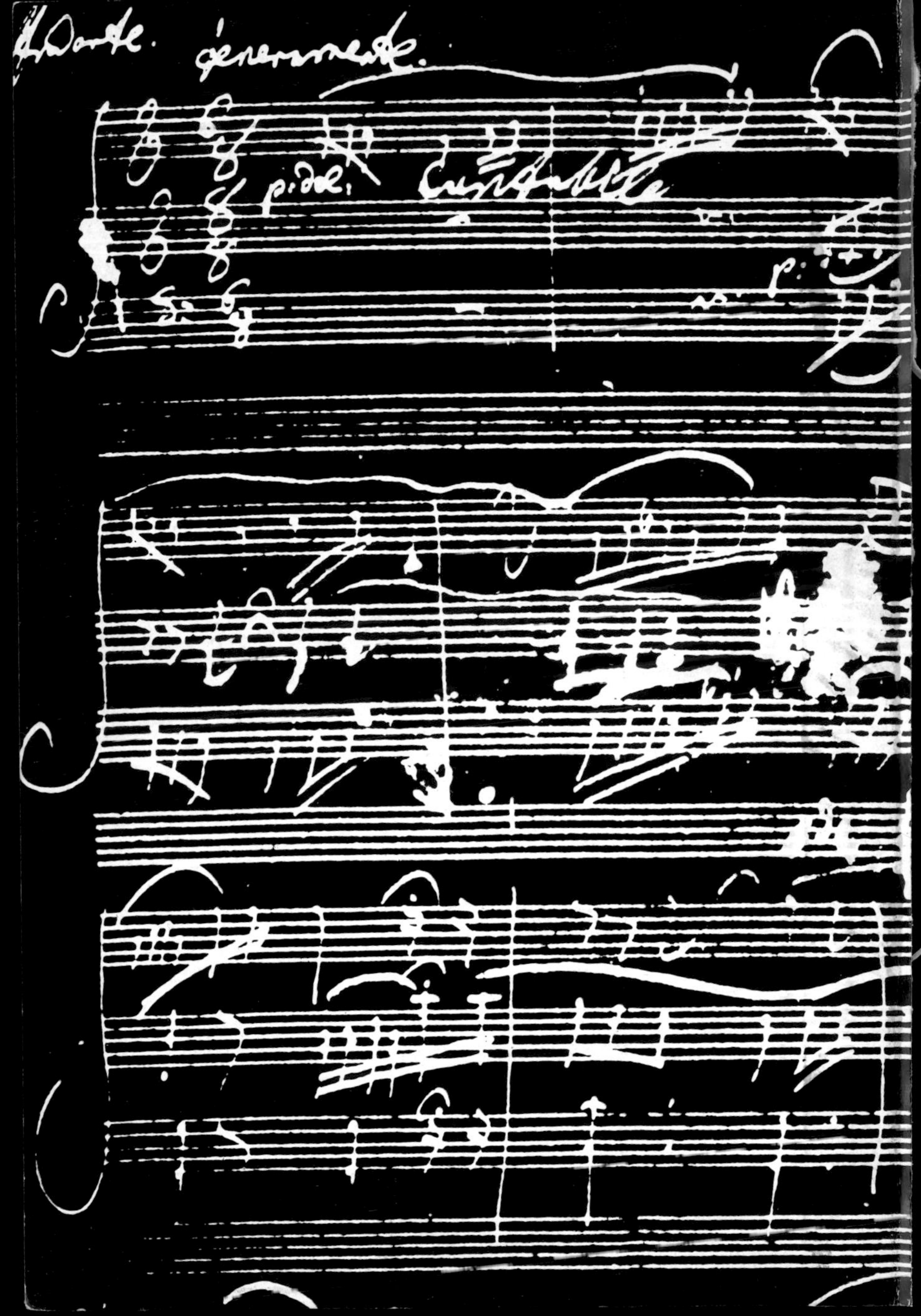
cantabile

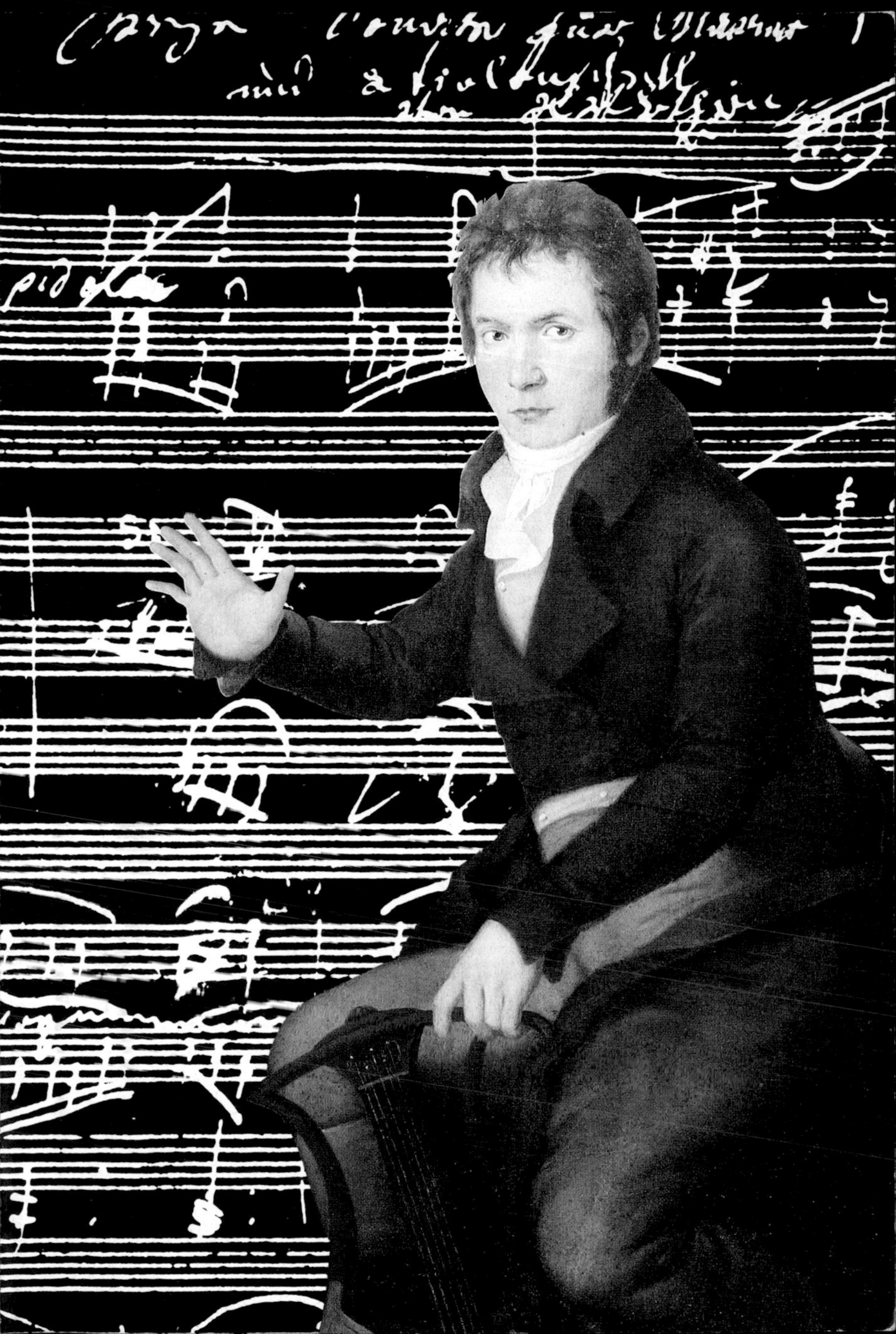

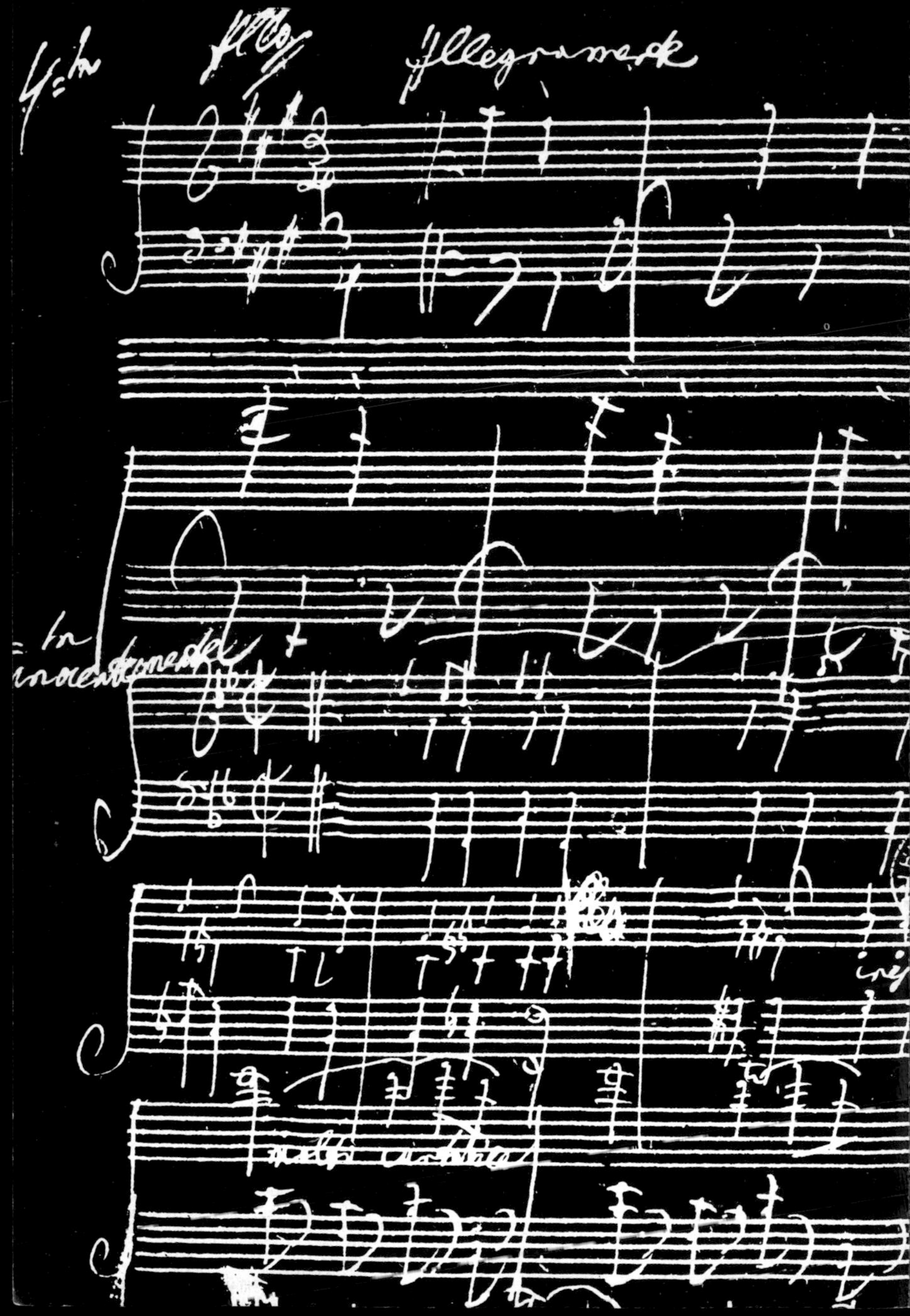

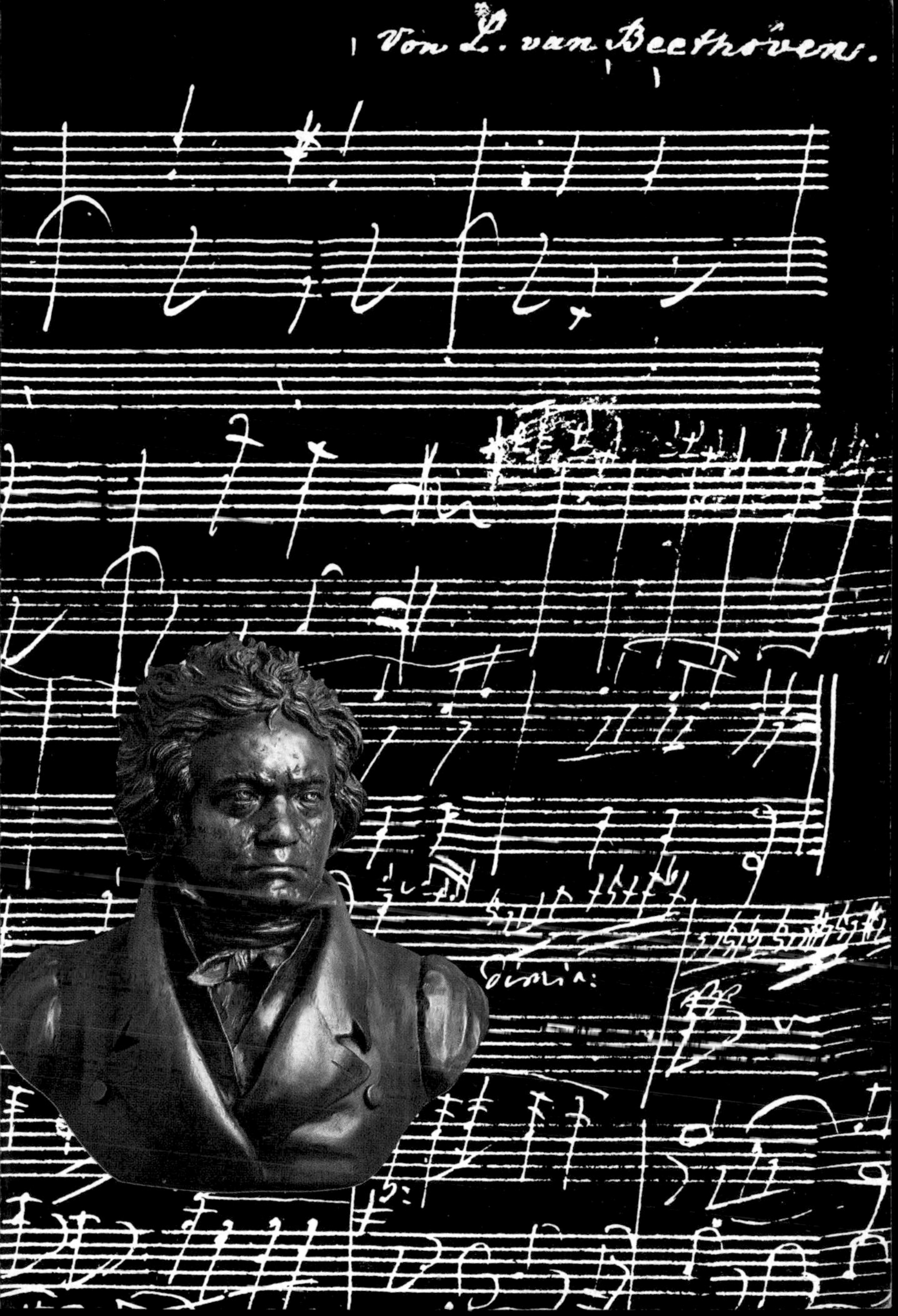
Von L. van Beethoven.

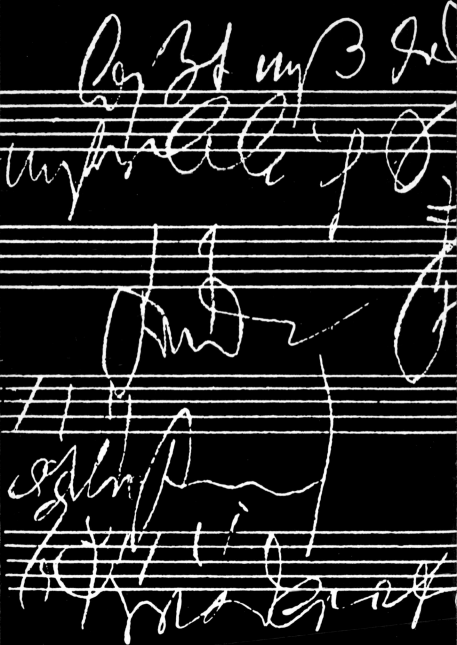

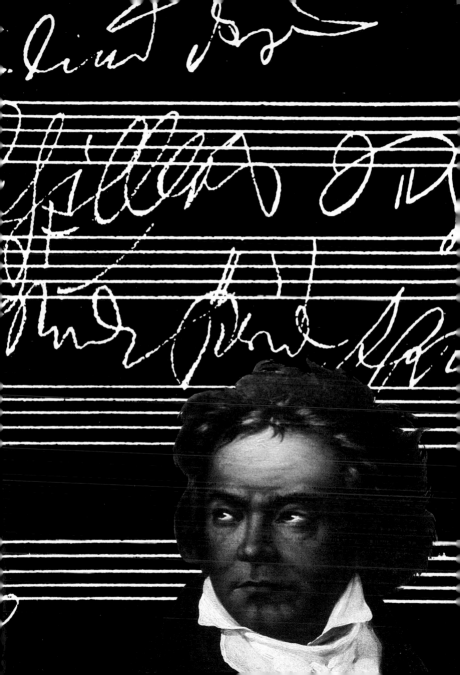

CONTENTS

BEETHOVEN
THE COMPOSER AS HERO

Philippe A. Autexier

DISCOVERIES

HARRY N. ABRAMS, INC., PUBLISHERS

NEW YORK

In the 18th century the city of Bonn numbered more than ten thousand souls. Constructed in the French style by François de Cuvilliés and Balthasar Neumann, ornamented with spacious and beautiful gardens, the elegant German city prospered peacefully along the left bank of the Rhine. As with the cradle, so with the man: Beethoven would forever harbor within him Bonn's classical lines, the fine arrangement of its urban design.

CHAPTER I

PROMISE

"Nature is unaware of the detestable differences men place between themselves. She portions out the qualities of the heart without any preference for the nobility or the rich, and it even seems that natural perceptiveness be larger among common people than elsewhere.... A sensitive heart, how inestimable that is!"
G. E. Lessing, 1751

In 1268 the rebellious burghers of Cologne had forced their archbishop and elector (one of the princes entitled to choose the Holy Roman emperor) out of the city. The court was moved to the small neighboring town of Bonn, where it would remain until 1794, when it was occupied during the French Revolution. Having become a princely residence in the Holy Roman Empire—a loose confederation of several European territories, including Germany, Austria, and Bohemia—Bonn was soon peopled by courtiers, functionaries, servants, and small businessmen.

More a Court than a City

Bonn's artistic and cultural life particularly benefited from its new status. Operas were mounted to honor notables visiting the town or to celebrate carnivals. Oratorios marked Lent, and cantatas embellished all manner of occasions. Instrumental music began to enliven secular daily life as well as being a staple of concerts at court. Yet no artist of renown would think of settling down permanently in this backwater, even though it was the capital of one of the largest electoral principalities of the Holy Roman Empire, which had jurisdiction over much of northern Germany and parts of Holland and Belgium.

Beethoven kept the portrait of his grandfather (left) above his desk.

Preceding pages: *View of Bonn and the Prince's Residence* and *Beethoven at Thirty.*

Nonetheless, it was here that the Flemish singer Ludwig van Beethoven (1712–73)—grandfather of the composer—took up residence starting in 1732. He was given a one-year trial without payment as a singer in the chapel at court, that is, in the small musical ensemble maintained by the archbishop-prince. At the end of the year he was easily able to secure a long-term position, with the relatively high yearly salary of 400 florins.

In the 18th century it was common for children to enter into the same profession as their parents. So it was that Ludwig van Beethoven trained his son Johann (1740–92) for a career in music. In 1758 Johann, in his turn, was engaged for the chapel. Ludwig became *Kapellmeister* (the musical director of the court or of a church) in 1761 and hoped that Johann, with his facility on the violin and in singing as well as his knowledge of the harpsichord, would someday follow him. Meanwhile, Johann, with wages of only 100 florins (the finances of the elector no longer allowed him the generosity from which Ludwig had benefited thirty years earlier), had to make up the difference by giving singing and violin lessons to the town's well-to-do families. In 1767 he married Maria Magdalena Keverich (1746–87), a young widow originally from Trier. When her husband later turned increasingly to drink, she proved a stabilizing influence for her family.

Confronted more harshly than his grandfather with the realities of daily life, Ludwig's parents (in medallions) did not impress on him moral and social ideals but rather a sense of the unremitting struggle for existence. The city of Bonn (above), however, proved a civilizing influence.

On 17 December 1770 Ludwig Was Baptized in the Saint Remigius Parish Church in Bonn

The infant was probably born either that day or the day before, although no documents remain to confirm the fact. He was named after his grandfather, who was also his godfather. As soon as the child was able to walk, the Kapellmeister would take him on strolls down city streets and through the gardens of the palace. Perhaps he already imagined his grandson assuming a place in the line of Beethoven Kapellmeisters. Unhappily, he never had the opportunity to watch young Beethoven's first musical efforts; shortly after the child's third birthday, the old man passed away. Maria Magdalena, who cherished his memory with great fondness, soon transformed Ludwig the elder into a mythic figure, symbol of a happier time, vanished forever, and she imparted her attitude to her son.

During that period, the archbishop-prince's musical ensemble included twelve string players, two bassoonists, an organist, and nine singers, not to mention the small guardsmen's band. Kapellmeister Johann van Beethoven was soon forced to yield its direction to the Italian Andrea Lucchesi, who offered the additional advantage of being a composer and director of an opera troupe. In 1774 Johann's second surviving son, Caspar Carl, was born, and a third, Johann, followed two years later.

By his fifth year, little Ludwig was demonstrating musical leanings. Impressed by the example of Leopold Mozart, who had already been touring throughout Europe with his musical-prodigy son Wolfgang for a decade, Johann decided to undertake the education of his

Beethoven was baptized on 17 December 1770 (opposite below). Music inhabited his childhood home in Bonn (opposite above), but not in the form of an angelic choir, as popular imagination would have it (above)—rather, his father's daily practicing and lessons to pupils who did not always play in tune. Happily, there was chamber music among professional friends.

son with the same objectives in mind. But Ludwig seemed impervious to his father's efforts. He preferred to play alone on his instrument, improvising, against his father's express order.

At seven he began attending elementary school, before entering the cathedral school, which would prepare him for the *gymnasium,* the secondary school. But he progressed much more rapidly with his music than he did in his studies; on 26 March 1778 his father presented him in concert in Cologne alongside one of his young female singing pupils.

After His First Concert, the Musical Education of the Young Beethoven Broadened

The archbishop-prince had become aware that he harbored a promising talent in his court. He decided to underwrite Beethoven's training and to entrust it to the finest musicians he employed.

The court organist, Heinrich van den Eeden, assisted by Tobias Friedrich Pfeiffer, was given the responsibility of teaching him the harpsichord; Franz Georg Rovantini, a relative of Maria Magdalena van Beethoven, took charge of his training on the violin. At church the child discovered the organ. He would sit at the foot of the organ loft, transfixed. Soon, as contemporary accounts relate, he was seen playing the six-o'clock mass at the church of Saint Remigius.

The organ fascinated young Beethoven. One of the organs he played as a child was that of Marienkirche (above). Apart from a Fugue in D (1783), he composed nothing for this instrument. However, the mystical atmosphere of the church (opposite, Saint Stephen's Cathedral in Vienna) permeated a number of his mature compositions.

"He plays the piano with much dexterity and strength," wrote Neefe (left) of his twelve-year-old pupil. "He sight-reads very well, and above all he plays J. S. Bach's *Well-Tempered Clavier*...the *non plus ultra* of our art."

Meanwhile, life in Bonn continued as usual. The principal excitement each year centered around the theater, as the traveling dramatic troupes would stay in town only for two or three seasons. Posters for 1781 announced a production of *Adelheit von Veltheim*, an opera with a Turkish setting, its "harem" subject almost identical to Mozart's *Abduction from the Seraglio*. The troupe's musical director, Christian Gottlob Neefe, wrote the highly successful score.

Neefe won so much acclaim at court that when the organist, van den Eeden, died that year Neefe was asked to take on the post. At the same time he became overseer of young Beethoven's musical education.

The new master put an end to the child's old-school training. Neefe had been influenced by the ideals of the Enlightenment. He valued methodical, organized thought, and his interests ranged from literature to politics, from music to Freemasonry. He was also one of the principal organizers of the Order of the Illuminati in Bonn, a rationalist society. All this implies that Beethoven was imbued early on with the humanitarian values that characterized a large part of his later music.

Neefe's teaching methods resembled those of Leopold Mozart twenty years earlier with his son Wolfgang: First, shape the child's musical taste by exposing him straightaway to the finest composers. Neefe relied on the unerring values of the Viennese school—as had Leopold Mozart, while also including the contemporary Joseph Haydn. And, good northern German Protestant that he was, he included the compositions of fellow northern Germans Johann Sebastian and Carl Philipp Emanuel Bach. *The Well-*

Beethoven was to be a pianist. But, for the time being, his education took place primarily on the organ and harpsichord, which were both limited in their dynamic expression, or the nuances of loudness and softness. On the other hand, these two instruments could create distinctly different timbres, allowing him to gain a profound grasp of "voices," that is, the different parts that make up a composition.

Beethoven's first *Three Sonatas* (below) were published in 1783.

Tempered Clavier provided the ideal material for a lively study of counterpoint.

Soon, Neefe was able to involve Beethoven in the musical life of the court. In 1782 the young Ludwig became the harpsichord player for the orchestra—an important post, as the harpsichord was the center, the soul, of the 18th-century orchestra. And he not only held the position of orchestral director for the opera, he also served as accompanist for all the recitatives. This experience as harpsichordist could only further enrich the knowledge of the young musician, especially in the area of harmony.

First Compositions

Beethoven's first compositions, all for keyboard, were not long in coming. "Nine Variations on a March by Dressler" appeared in late 1782, and in October 1783 Bossler, an important publisher in Speyer, on the Rhine, published *Three Sonatas* dedicated to the archbishop-prince. Themes appear in these three sonatinas that would resurface in Beethoven's work some years later.

During the second half of the 18th century the pianoforte—the first version of the modern piano—almost completely replaced the harpsichord (above, a Donzelague harpsichord of 1716). The new instrument facilitated contrasts, from a barely audible *pianissimo* to a violent *fortissimo*—which would prove a fundamental aspect of Beethoven' style.

Maximilian Franz (left) emulated his brother Emperor Joseph II by cultivating the arts, especially music.

The enjoyment of music in Beethoven's day was much more a private affair, within the salons, than a public one. People would sing together at the piano or play sonatas—on occasion, accompanied by flute or violin—and, in the most enthusiastic circles, even play string quartets. Joseph Haydn (above, at the piano, and left, playing the violin) carried the genre to the highest point of refinement, which assured him the favor of the "true connoisseurs," according to the expression of the age. Mozart and Beethoven also accorded a major part of their work to chamber music, above all, to the string quartet.

These first sparks of creativity were restricted to the somewhat simple sphere of the rondo and theme-and-variation; clearly, they were heavily influenced by the contemporary masters the young composer had studied or heard during recent years—C. P. E. Bach, Joseph Haydn, the Abbé Sterkel, who was very much in vogue in Paris at the time, and, of course, Neefe.

Beethoven began composing at the very moment that the liberal bent of the Enlightenment was strongly influencing the political and intellectual life of Bonn. The archbishop-prince to whom the *Three Sonatas* had been dedicated died on 15 April 1784. Elected as his successor was Maximilian Franz of Hapsburg, archduke of Austria, the youngest brother of Emperor Joseph II, head of the Holy Roman Empire. A great music lover, Maximilian Franz had been friendly with Mozart in Vienna. Indeed, it was thought that he intended to invite him to Bonn.

Following in the footsteps of Joseph II, Maximilian Franz enlarged the small academy created during the reign of his predecessor and turned it into a university. Beethoven himself, in 1789, attended its courses on Immanuel Kant's philosophy. Maximilian Franz' liberal ideas encouraged supporters of the Enlightenment to venture from the shadows under which they had lived for some time. Neefe dissolved the lodge of the Order of the Illuminati, replacing it with a reading society open to a larger public, which promoted ideas of the Enlightenment and works of modern literature. Most of Beethoven's friends attended the reading society more or less regularly.

Beethoven Obtains His First Salaried Post at Court in Bonn

Maximilian Franz took an active role in the cultural life at court, just as his brother Joseph did in Vienna. In June 1784 he dismissed the theatrical society and sought a general report on the situation of his staff. In it,

Johann van Beethoven was described as a poor man who was losing his voice and whose behavior was barely adequate. His son Ludwig, described as skillful at his art, had replaced Lucchesi at the organ. His conduct was rated as honorable, but he was receiving no salary. The archbishop-prince reduced Johann's salary by 15 florins but awarded his son 150 florins annually and assigned him the position of second organist.

As Ludwig progressed in his musical career, his father surrendered increasingly to his taste for wine. One by one, his pupils left him. Home life became painful. When he was able, Ludwig took refuge in the home of friends, above all, the Wegelers and the von Breunings, enlightened members of Bonn high society, to whom he would remain loyal to his last days.

"Keep an eye on that one—some day he will give the world some thing to talk about!" Mozart reportedly said of the young Ludwig (above).

The arts in Vienna flourished under the enlightened rule of Emperor Joseph II (opposite). His brother, Maximilian Franz, brought the same attitude to Bonn after he was elected archbishop-prince in 1784.

It was Maximilian Franz' fervent desire to raise the level of musical culture at court. To that end he decided to send Ludwig to Vienna to study with Mozart. Vienna was, for the young musician, "the best place in the world," as Mozart himself had written six years earlier; it boasted the finest musicians, concerts, and theaters.

In the imperial capital Beethoven played for Mozart and may have received a lesson or two, but in April 1787, only two weeks after his arrival, he returned home on learning that his mother had fallen gravely ill. Maria Magdalena died on 17 July.

In his younger years (above), Beethoven was renowned above all as an extraordinary improviser.

Several months later young Count Ferdinand von Waldstein, from Vienna, arrived in Bonn. Member of the Teutonic Order, passionate about music, and an occasional composer himself, he knew Mozart in Vienna. In the salons of Bonn he admired Beethoven's improvisations on the piano. Waldstein brought the radiance of Vienna to his new friend. For the young musician's own life was darkening; his father, Johann, was falling into complete alcoholic disgrace. Ludwig became aware that he had become bread-winner for his family. In November 1789 he received a decree from the elector allowing him to assume the role of head of the family, and to receive half of his father's salary.

Beethoven and his piano pupil Eleonore von Breuning, nicknamed Lorchen (below right; her mother is at left), were by no means indifferent to one another. "O that your happiness could completely match my own! this year, then, it will attain its supreme aim," she wrote to her teacher.

But she married a mutual friend, Franz Wegeler, to whom Beethoven admitted in 1826, "I still have Lorchen's silhouette; I tell you that so that you see how dear to me is all the love and happiness of my youth."

More and More, Bonn Seemed to Emulate Vienna

During the seasons of 1789 and 1790, operas by the most prominent composers on the European scene—André-Ernest-Modeste Grétry, Antonio Salieri, Georg Anton Benda—were being performed, as were the masterworks of Mozart: *The Abduction from the Seraglio, The Marriage of Figaro,* and *Don Giovanni.*

In February 1790, however, the theatrical season was

Vienna lived for the theater; above, the Leopold theater in that city. The new elector wanted it to be the same in Bonn. He only programmed proven works to insure that they were of the highest quality.

interrupted to mourn the death of Joseph II. Neefe's reading society took advantage of this occasion to commission Beethoven to produce a "Cantata on the Death of Emperor Joseph II." This was followed by a cantata marking Leopold II's accession to the throne. Neither was ever performed.

Yet at least one of these 1790 cantatas was shown to Joseph Haydn when he traveled through Bonn in 1792 on his way back from his first sojourn in London. Maximilian Franz accepted the elderly master's proposal to take the young composer as pupil and sent Beethoven back to Vienna in early November 1792.

Before Ludwig's departure Count Waldstein gave him a bundle of letters of introduction to his Viennese friends and relatives. In the imperial capital, where Mozart had died less than a year earlier, music was everywhere. Four or five orchestras and numerous theaters strived for audiences. The piano reigned supreme. The best families, whether noble or bourgeois, nurtured chamber music. Each year the Musicians' Society gave a huge concert to benefit widows and orphans in which almost all of the city's two hundred professional musicians participated. Indeed, music, theater, and opera were almost able to make the Viennese forget that war had just begun: The armies of the French Revolution were just then storming Germany.

The "Great Mogul" —as Joseph Haydn (below) called his pupil Beethoven—proved to be a demanding and independent disciple. The master-teacher was not equal to the task of training a musician who already knew what he wanted—and who, in the final count, could get it just as well on his own.

In 1793 Beethoven took up quarters in the residence of Prince Karl von Lichnowsky, a distant relative of Count Waldstein and close friend of the late Mozart. The prince organized chamber music performances in his home, with three excellent musicians participating: violinist Ignaz Schuppanzigh, violist Franz Weiss, and cellist Nikolaus Kraft. For this reason chamber music forms the most important part of Beethoven's first works in Vienna.

CHAPTER II
THE PATH TO ISOLATION

"Do all the good you can, love liberty above all; and, whether it be before a royal throne, never betray the truth!"
Beethoven, 1792

His lessons with Haydn began without delay, but Beethoven felt a lack of rigor in the teaching of the old master. He decided to take additional lessons, in secret, with Johann Schenk, then with the organist Johann Georg Albrechtsberger. Antonio Salieri, meanwhile, gave him free introductory lessons to vocal music and Italian prosody.

Haydn, when he learned of Beethoven's secret lessons, took offense at having to compete with Schenk and appeared critical of his student's latest compositions. Beethoven interpreted Haydn's remarks as signs of jealousy. The dispute grew more intense when Haydn showed Maximilian Franz, as evidence of his pupil's progress, compositions written well before Beethoven's departure from Bonn. The elector recognized them and became angry. In March 1794 he stopped payments for the education of his protégé.

Yet Beethoven was not left destitute. In the salons of Vienna he was overwhelmingly popular, just as Mozart had been twelve years earlier. In addition, he gave plenty of piano lessons. But the cutting of his funds forced him to make a head-on assault of the musical scene; the salons of the well-to-do would not suffice.

Taking on the Public

In 1795 Beethoven, as composer and performer, appeared before Viennese audiences. First he took part in the large Musicians' Society benefit concert on 29 March, playing piano in a concerto of his own

P receding pages: *Beethoven's Drawing Room in Vienna,* in 1827, and detail of the painting *The Last Chord.*

BEETHOVEN

Oeuvre 1re composition, no doubt an early version of the piece later known as the Piano Concerto no. 2 in B-flat Major.

Then he negotiated with Carlo Artaria, the largest music publisher in Vienna, for the publication of his Three Trios for Piano, Violin, and Violoncello, op. 1, developed during the chamber music sessions at Prince Lichnowsky's. Music lovers flocked to subscribe to the edition of the *Three Trios.* Beethoven still attended the salons of Vienna with as much frequency as ever, but he might refuse to sit down at the keyboard; even the most

Antonio Salieri (opposite below), one of Beethoven's teachers, and Carlo Artaria (left), an early publisher of Beethoven's music (opposite above, the Three Piano Trios, op. 1), often heard at Prince Lichnowsky's salons (above).

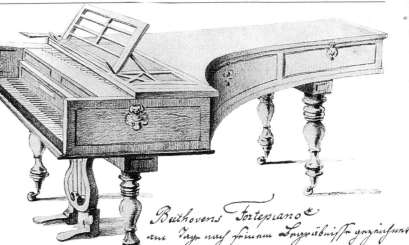

Beethovens Fortepiano
eine Tage nach seinem Dungrübniße gezeichnet

ardent entreaties had little
effect. "It is fine to spend time with the aristocracy," he
wrote his friend Baron Nikolaus Zmeskall, "but one also
has to know how to gain their respect." This, however,
didn't prevent him from writing dance pieces for small
orchestra for the salons.

All his compositions from this period involved piano,
and most were piano solos. Beethoven's musical thought
was intimately tied to his instrument, and the public
expected virtuosity from him or works that put virtuoso
playing at the forefront. In this spirit, the piano
dominates the Quintet in E-flat Major, op. 16,
throughout; in this veritable concerto, four wind
instruments take the place of an entire orchestra.

The string trio gave Beethoven the first chance to
free himself of the keyboard. He first reworked the Trio
in E-flat Major, op. 3, written shortly before leaving
Bonn, then wrote a Serenade in D Major, op. 18 (1796),
and Three String Trios, op.
9 (1797). The last of
these, a particularly
successful work, already
hints at the lyricism of the
late string quartets.

Celebrated as a pianist
from his earliest
years in Vienna,
Beethoven received many
instruments in homage to
his talents from manufac-
turers or personalities who
admired him. Conrad
Graf of Vienna made him
a piano more powerful
than most (opposite).
The large Broadwood
piano (above) was given
him just before his death
by Ferdinand Ries, John
Cramer, and George
Smart, all of them well
known in the London
musical scene of the
1820s. Smart conducted
the English premiere of
the Ninth Symphony.

* aus dem Fabrik des M.ᵉ Broadwood in London
meir F.H. Fermd. Ries
  „ John Cramer   { als Geschenk übergeben
S.ʳ Georg Smart   in J. 1820.

Composer Ignaz von Seyfried vividly described Beethoven at the piano: "His playing dashed along at full tilt like a waterfall frothing wildly.... Then, it eased, exhausted, exhaling a slight moan, dissolving into melancholy."
Opposite above, *Beethoven Composing the Moonlight Sonata*; opposite below, *Beethoven Playing for His Close Friends*; and left, *Beethoven Playing for Prince Louis Ferdinand of Prussia*. Below, a page from the manuscript of the *Moonlight* Sonata.

The young harpsichordist from Bonn had become an experienced musician. He had the support of a handful of aristocratic patrons who were more at his service than he at theirs. These were the happiest years of his life. He had conquered Vienna, and now he dreamed of enlarging his empire. Prague and Berlin acclaimed him, in awe of the violence and originality of his playing, as well as the strangeness of his ideas.

But he never abandoned himself to the seductions of pure virtuosity. The spectacular but rather empty grandiosity fostered by his pianist colleagues Abbé Joseph Gelinek and Joseph Wölfl, following the example of Muzio Clementi, was not enough for him. The era of the virtuoso had begun, but Beethoven wanted nothing of it, except insofar as it could serve his musical intentions.

Composer, Nothing but a Composer

Just as Mozart had in the 1780s, Beethoven soon gave himself completely to composition. This was made obvious by his attitude onstage when he played piano—when he was not improvising, he performed only his own compositions.

Grande Sonate pathétique
Pour le Clavecin ou Piano Forte
Composée et dédiée
A Son Altesse Monseigneur le Prince
CHARLES DE LICHNOWSKY
par
Louis Van Beethoven
Oeuvre 13.
Bey Joseph Eder am Graben.

He did not stop giving piano lessons to young pupils from the aristocracy or the wealthy Viennese bourgeoisie, but all his activities had in view the goal of allowing him to compose without hindrances. Getting up at dawn, he would write until one o'clock in the afternoon. He produced at least ten sonatas for solo piano (among them the celebrated *Pathétique*, op. 13) and the Six String Quartets, op. 18, dedicated to Prince Lobkowitz, as well as trios; sonata duets, a greatly popular Septet for Winds and Strings, op. 20, two concertos for piano and orchestra, and a symphony—all during the last six years of the 18th century.

Already Beethoven was leaving the stamp of his personal style on the music he wrote. Ideas poured forth in a tumult he could barely control. They suggested violent dynamic and rhythmic oppositions, and they seemed to stretch to the breaking point the very framework of the composition; Beethoven needed space to calm his anguish at not having said everything. He seemed to want to seize every occasion to take an unexpected path, always delivering more than the conventional. Instead of going directly to the point he would indulge the caprices of his imagination and his eccentric discoveries. Happily, his mastery of contrasts allowed him to avoid the incongruity that might have resulted from this approach. Haydn had the impression that his old pupil was merely continuing to improvise and write fantasies. He no longer understood him.

Václav Tomašek wrote in his 1845 autobiography, "That which is singular and original seems to be his principal aim in terms of compositional material." (The *Pathétique* Sonata, opposite left, and the third String Quartet, op. 18, above.) Berlin and Prague (opposite right) found his ideas both strange and fascinating.

Beethoven Altered the Very Structure of Music

In the past, tempo had been the dominating force: Measure and melody, metric and rhythmic pulsation were inextricably linked. Mozart

A *Music Lesson*

had succeeded in liberating music from the ascendancy of "time" by associating it with "space," by awarding to the pitch of instruments and notes an importance overlooked until then; the coupling of space with time—that is, movement—forms the basis of his works. When he died, composers connected with the French Revolution, above all, François-Joseph Gossec, with his "Marche Lugubre" (1792), were abandoning the principle of thematic development. They tended to construct their music around independent motifs that were not directly linked one to the next. In this way they freed themselves from both time and action, and their motifs became what may be called gestures.

Beethoven followed this development but rejected the idea that the simple juxtaposition of contrasting gestures was enough to create the form of a piece. He preferred to vary his musical motifs, to rework them, accentuating their

"May assiduous work make you receive Mozart's spirit from the hands of Haydn," Count Waldstein wrote Beethoven (below) in 1792, as the young musician prepared to return to Vienna. His farewell wish proved prophetic, as Beethoven was to join the pantheon of musical greats (opposite above): Bach, Haydn, and Mozart.

characteristics one after the next, to give them different shadings and to bring them into contrasting relations with one another until he had created the sense of development.

In contrast to action, the gesture overcomes external shackles. It is pure and absolute, like a Kantian imperative. The very beginning of the *Pathétique* Sonata is a gesture. It is self-contained, and the development it experiences during the course of the piece is linked neither to its past nor to an action. Alone, this gesture, reminiscent of an idealized march, engenders pathos by means of the power it brings to bear on the changing states of a soul in conflict. It becomes the symbol of the struggle of humanity against its fate.

Destiny Knocks at Beethoven's Door

He sensed he was losing his hearing. The first difficulties appeared in 1794. By the end of the century his auditory faculties had weakened to such an extent that Beethoven began avoiding society. It seemed to him impossible that a musician be known to be deaf. By 1801 he could no longer hear high-pitched vocal and instrumental sounds. To understand a theater piece, he had to sit extremely close to the stage, and his ears buzzed into the night. However, he claimed his malady did not bother him when he composed or played. He even considered undertaking concert tours.

As he avoided speaking, and as he did not respond when called to at any distance, he gained a reputation for being surly, even misanthropic. Added to the loss of his hearing, this deterioration of his relationship with society plunged him into severe periods of depression. When he visited the village of Heiligenstadt, outside

"In music as in painting and even in the written word, which is however the most definite of the arts, there is always an empty space filled in by the imagination of the listener."

Charles Baudelaire
1861

B*eethoven Composing*

Vienna, on 6 and 10 October, he was plagued by suicidal impulses of such violence that he took up pen and paper to give himself relief in a letter addressed to his two brothers. This document became known as the "Heiligenstadt Testament."

"Your Beethoven is leading a very unhappy life and is at variance with nature and his Creator. Many times already I have cursed him for exposing his creatures to the slightest hazard, so that the most beautiful blossom is thereby often crushed and destroyed. Let me tell you that my most prized possession, my hearing, has greatly deteriorated. When you were still with me, I already felt the symptoms; but I said nothing about them. Now they have become very much worse. We must wait and see whether my hearing can be restored. The symptoms are said to be caused by the condition of my bowels. So far as the latter are concerned, I am almost quite cured. But that my hearing too will improve, I must hope, it is true, but I hardly think it possible, for diseases of that kind are the most difficult to cure. You realize what a sad life I must now lead." Letter to Karl Amenda June 1801

Beethoven Composing

His undiminished drive to keep working came to his rescue. "I will brave destiny," he wrote to a friend sometime after June 1801, for it was then he finally decided to reveal his secret to a few people. Marked by these obsessions with death and suicide, the music of this period is often saturated with a lugubrious quality. Sometimes an entire movement will be imbued with it. Indeed, it is a funeral march that ends the Sonata in A-flat Major, op. 26 (1801), and Beethoven specified that he intended it to be about "the death of a hero"— probably none other than himself. Happily, he received more commissions than he could execute, to the degree that work compensated him for the tragedy he felt in his innermost heart. Publishers fought for his works and paid any price he asked.

Beginning in 1800 the ever-faithful Prince Lichnowsky granted Beethoven an additional annual stipend of 600 florins, to allow him to devote himself completely to composing. Thus, the first three years of the 19th century saw the appearance of the Symphony no. 2 in

Heiligenstadt was one of those rustic spots that Beethoven would love all his life for their serenity and peacefulness (above, *Beethoven in Front of His House in Heiligenstadt*). At the outset, work to do: the Second Symphony was on the drawing board, and Ferdinand Ries came from Vienna to take lessons. But by the end of the summer, Beethoven was no longer able to hear a shepherd's flute in the woods.

D Major, Piano Concerto no. 3 in C Minor, six sonatas for piano and violin (opp. 23, 24, 30, and 47), seven sonatas for solo piano (opp. 26, 27, 28, and 31), and a ballet *(The Creatures of Prometheus)*. This music was all of a heightened power and concentration.

Beethoven's art profited from the suffering life had inflicted on him. His destiny and his music took on a heroic aspect.

Love, When You Hold Me!

In May 1789 Baron Zmeskall introduced Beethoven to the Brunsvik family under the pretext that the young countesses had need of a good piano tutor. Interwoven with the pointers on keyboard technique was a tapestry of tender regards, languid sighs, half-phrases, and ambiguous messages.

Therese, the eldest, was twenty-four; her education and intelligence were dazzling, as was her idealism, but she was not beautiful. Of a more restless character, and younger by four years, her sister Josephine had married against her will in June 1799 the aged Count Joseph Deym—who raised little protest against Beethoven's almost daily visits.

But it was their cousin Giulietta Guicciardi's fresh beauty that overwhelmed Beethoven. "She loves me and I love her," he wrote to a friend in November 1801. "For two years, I have once again known some blissful moments, and for the first time I've had the sense that marriage can make someone happy; alas, she is not in the same social situation as I and, for the moment, I truly cannot marry."

He dedicated to Giulietta the second sonata "quasi una fantasia," op. 27, no. 2, known as the *Moonlight*. But

Princess Christiane, *née* Thun (opposite), like her husband, Prince Lichnowsky, admired Beethoven's music. The Sonata for Piano and Violin, op. 12, above.

This ivory medallion depicting a young woman was found among Beethoven's papers at his death. Is it Giulietta Guicciardi or the youngest of the Brunsvik sisters, Charlotte?

"For you, there is no longer happiness, except in yourself, through your art. Oh God! Give me the strength to overcome myself! Nothing, from now on, should bind me to life. In this way, everything is finished with A."

Beethoven, 1812

Concerning the "Immortal Beloved," conjectures have centered principally around Giulietta Guicciardi and her cousins the Brunsviks (Therese is pictured at left). Additional candidates are the Berlin singer Amalie Sebald (opposite) and Antonie and Bettina Brentano. Other women in his life were Anna Van Westerholt (above left), whom he knew when he was a young man in Bonn, and Julie von Breuning (above).

Giulietta married the handsome Count Gallenberg in November 1803 and left for Naples.

Less than three months later, Count Deym died, leaving Josephine pregnant with their fourth child. Beethoven redoubled his attentions to her, but the young widow felt bound above all by her maternal duties. He persisted. She wrote to him at the beginning of 1805: "An inexpressible feeling that lies at the bottom of my soul has made me love you. Before I knew you, your music carried me away with enthusiasm for you. Your goodness of character and your fondness for me have done the rest. The favor you have accorded me, the pleasure of your visits would have been the most beautiful jewel of my life, if only you loved me in a less physical manner. Do not berate me if I cannot respond to this physical love. I would have to break sacred bonds were I to follow your entreaties. Please believe that I suffer the more in fulfilling my duties and that my actions are certainly guided by noble intentions."

"I was loved by her very much, and more than her husband ever was," Beethoven was said to have told his first biographer, Anton Schindler, concerning Giulietta Guicciardi. The break, before this beloved woman's marriage, was a shock for him. Shortly afterward, while staying in Vienna, Giulietta searched Beethoven out. "But I scorned her," he told Schindler. "If I had wasted my vital forces in that way, what would have been left for the best and most noble of myself?"

By 1803 Beethoven Was a Composer in the Forefront

Publishers clamored for his works. But his reputation depended for the most part on his chamber music and solo piano works. He had written no operas, no oratorios; the few symphonic or concert pieces he had written were not yet impressive. Mozart and Haydn continued to reign as masters of the orchestral world and the lyric stage. There, also, Beethoven was to make his presence felt.

Poet Ludwig Rellstab saw in the "Sonata quasi una fantasia," op. 27, no. 2, "a boat in moonlight"—whence the nickname the *Moonlight* Sonata. Above left, a 1901 lithograph, *The Moonlight Sonata;* opposite, *Beethoven Playing the Moonlight Sonata for Giulietta Guicciardi.*

It was Emanuel Schikaneder who was to give Beethoven his chance to prove himself on the symphonic and lyric stage. Twelve years earlier, in his theater on the outskirts of town, he had premiered Mozart's last opera, *The Magic Flute*—whose libretto he had written as well as performed. This event attracted the cream of the Viennese public even to a location that remote. With the help of a wealthy merchant, he had just replaced his theater with a sumptuous hall with blue and gold decor. An elliptical plan allowed each of the six thousand spectators to gaze comfortably upon a stage of unusual size.

CHAPTER III
ORCHESTRA FIRST

"What Beethoven tosses your way is infinite."
Honoré de Balzac
Lettre à l'Etrangère
10 May 1834

Beethoven was the man of the hour. The nobility and wealthy bourgeoisie had been enthusiastically following his chamber music output for years. Schikaneder was sure that a poster with his name on it would attract this select audience, people who usually attended only the official theaters of the court. He signed Beethoven to a contract for a grand opera, *Vestas Feuer*, whose libretto he would write himself.

Preceding pages: *Performance of "The Creation" by J. Haydn in the Festival Hall of the Old University of Vienna in 1808* and a 19th-century oboe on the score and parts for the Ninth Symphony.

But First, Beethoven's Name Had to Be Linked with Symphonic and Vocal Music

Schikaneder suggested a major concert be staged that would feature, for the first time, only works by Beethoven. The date was set for 5 April 1803. The program included the two symphonies, the very new Piano Concerto no. 3 in C Minor, and various vocal works. Hastily, he also wrote a short oratorio, *The Mount of Olives,* which was meant to show off his ability for the forthcoming opera.

The morning of the concert, the general rehearsal started at eight o'clock. The program was so lengthy—indeed, it would not be given in its totality—that at half past two all the players were exhausted, yet they remained dissatisfied with the results. Prince Lichnowsky helped them recover their spirits by having baskets full of bread, butter, cold meats, and wine brought in; then he requested they rehearse the oratorio once more.

At six o'clock the theater was quite full. The orchestra played brilliantly. Paradoxically, it was Beethoven who disappointed the audience most, with his performance of the concerto. An ill-tempered critic did not miss the occasion to criticize the oratorio as well, citing its lack of expressivity, indeed, its superficiality. But the audience, for its part, greeted it with enthusiasm.

Henceforth, Beethoven Believed His Success Would Come by Way of the Opera and the Symphony

As usual, he was involved with several projects at the same time: a symphony already well along, the opera for Schikaneder, a piano sonata, and, most immediately, the Sonata in A Major for Piano and Violin, op. 47, a sort of violin concerto in which the piano takes the place of the orchestra.

Despite these projects he was in the process of finishing, Beethoven felt strapped in the Hapsburg capital. "Believe me, everyone around me has a

Emanuel Schikaneder was a talented actor and a colorful personality.

The Theater an der Wien (opposite) premiered *Fidelio,* the *Eroica* Symphony, the Violin Concerto in D Major, and the Sixth Symphony.

"This Kreutzer is a good, charming man whom I've had great pleasure in seeing during his stay here."
Beethoven

post and knows where his next meal is coming from; but my God, where to put a tiny talent like mine in the imperial court?"

He thought of traveling to Paris once he had finished his opera. Lichnowsky would go with him, and they would not be short of connections there. Just to make sure, he dedicated his last violin and piano sonata, the opus 47, to Rodolphe Kreutzer, "the premier violinist of Paris"—the derivation of this piece's name as the *Kreutzer* Sonata. (Although Beethoven had previously met Kreutzer when he came to Vienna on a visit and noted approvingly, "His simplicity and naturalness are much more agreeable to me than all the 'exterior' and 'interior' of most virtuosos," Kreutzer never played the sonata that has ever since carried his name.) And his next symphony, no. 3, would be a homage to Napoleon Bonaparte; he did not want it performed in Vienna

Even though Kreutzer refused to play the sonata composed on his behalf (frontispiece, above, shows the dedication), it blossomed under the bow of other virtuosos. The painting of 1900 above depicts a performance in an artist's studio in Paris.

before he left. In Napoleon, Beethoven saw, as many of his friends did, the man who had been able to free France from the bloody torments of the revolution without stifling its democratic ideals. In August 1804 the symphony was finished. But at the end of autumn, when Lichnowsky and his friend and pupil Ferdinand Ries told him that Napoleon was going to have himself crowned emperor of the French, he cried out, "Then he is nothing but an ordinary man! He is going to trample the rights of man underfoot and his ambition will make him the greatest of tyrants." Thereupon he scratched out Bonaparte's name on the title page of his manuscript.

The Third Symphony Proved "Imperial" in Stature, Though Not in Name

The style that had been evolving in the works of the last ten years culminated in this masterful work. In his own way, Beethoven attained heights that Napoleon could not reach. Beginning with the exposition in the opening Allegro con brio, each episode seemed to want to go off on its own and discover a new vista. In the symphony nothing is predictable, as the music constantly changes in a continuous evolution. The new title Beethoven chose, the *Eroica* (Heroic) Symphony, was perhaps more descriptive of the composition's character than its subject. In any case, the style itself took on a heroic cast.

Meanwhile, the *Vestas Feuer* project had fallen by the wayside. Beethoven had finished composing one scene,

Napoleon places the empress' crown on Josephine's head. This 1805–7 painting by Jacques-Louis David focusing on a gesture derives from the same aesthetic as Beethoven's music. But Napoleon's act displeased the composer. When he took the crown, Beethoven withdrew his dedication of the *Eroica* Symphony to him. He scratched out Napoleon's name on the manuscript title page (below).

but Schikaneder had been forced to resign as the theater's director. Although his contract for the opera had been renewed, Beethoven took advantage of the situation to suggest an opera on another subject, *Leonore or Conjugal Love,* by Jean-Nicolas Bouilly.

He devoted a good part of 1804 and 1805 to this lyric drama, which would take the name *Fidelio* at its premiere in November 1805. At the same time he finished the Triple Concerto for Piano, Violin, and Cello in C Major, as well as three piano sonatas (opp. 53, 54, and 57).

A Revolution in Timbre

Dedicated to Count Waldstein, the Piano Sonata in C Major, op. 53 (known as the *Aurora*), was as revolutionary for the piano as the *Eroica* Symphony had been for the orchestra. Beethoven used all the notes that he was able to play on the keyboard of the splendid piano that instrument-maker Sébastien Erard had sent him from Paris in 1803. From the outset the sonata exploits the contrast between the extremes of highs and lows. A rapid tremolo of a C-major chord rumbles in the bass. Noise or music? It is difficult to tell—until something escapes from this distant and chaotic universe in the treble notes like a ray of light. And this light,

Instead of the customary arrangement of three strings per note, the piano constructed for Beethoven by Conrad Graf of Vienna (below) has four strings, giving a much more powerful sound. It was long believed that Graf added the extra string to compensate for the composer's deafness. In fact, he had built other pianos along the same lines before this.

"In the course of a walk," recalled Ferdinand Ries, "during which time we became lost, to the point of not getting back to Döbling until eight o'clock, Beethoven hummed the whole way and sometimes started to shout out tones without, however, singing. On arriving back, he set to work on the finale of the Sonata in F Minor"—the *Appassionata*. (Below, a passage from the first movement.) Beethoven is pictured playing it on a Polish postcard of about 1910, above.

finally, illuminates the entire work.

In contrast to this exuberant music, the Piano Sonata in F Minor, op. 57 (the *Appassionata*), explores the most intimate corners of Beethoven's inner landscape. Anxiety, torment, violence, and tenacity: The right hand ascends even higher than it did in the C-major sonata, all the way up to the highest C. At the end of the piece, the right hand repeats this culminating note with a fury of sixteenth notes, when the left hand suddenly plunges the work into a cavernous depth. Until Beethoven, volume and expressive power were linked to harmonic functions. With Mozart, they had begun to

Scenes from *Fidelio*

Left: Leonore, disguised as a young man under the name of Fidelio, interrupts at the moment when Pizarro, the tyrannical governor, wants to kill Florestan, her husband (quartet no. 16 from the 1806 version).

Page 58, above: Rocco, Florestan's jailer, notices his daughter Marzelline's love for Fidelio, whom he has just hired (quartet in canon form, no. 4, from the 1806 version).

Page 58, below: Pizarro decides to satisfy his thirst for revenge against Florestan (aria with chorus, no. 6, from the 1806 version)

Page 59, above: Pizarro orders Rocco to dig quickly Florestan's grave (duet, no. 7, from the 1806 version).

Page 59, below: Florestan, who hasn't eaten for two days, drinks a little of Rocco's wine, and as he regains his strength, Leonore's heart beats with joy—and with anguish, because his grave is now ready.

Rocco:„ Sie liebt ihn, es ist klar. Ja, Mädchen, er wird dein."

Pizarro:„ Die Rache werd'ich kühlen."

Pizarro: „Du gräbst in der Cisterne, sehr schnell für ihn ein Grab."

Leonore: „Wie heftig pochet mir das Herz."

assume a life of their own. But it was Beethoven who bestowed on them a true independence, making them new dimensions of musical language.

November 1805: The Moment of *Fidelio*'s Premiere

The climate for opera was hardly propitious: Vienna was under military occupation for the first time since the Ottoman siege of 1683, and its inhabitants, living under the threat of Napoleon's army, attended performances without having the heart for it. The preparation for and rehearsal of theatrical productions was fraught with obstacles—if the actors had not simply left town already. To Beethoven the public's reservations about the *Eroica* Symphony already augured badly. The first performances of *Fidelio* failed. Beethoven immediately sat down to do a revision of his opera; this was staged with no greater success at the end of March 1806.

A return to instrumental music seemed in order. In this realm, everyone agreed, Beethoven excelled. One by one, he wrote the Three Quartets, op. 59, dedicated to the Russian ambassador, Prince Razumovsky, the Symphony no. 4 in B-flat Major, and the Violin Concerto in D Major. It seemed as though his deafness had temporarily

The colored engraving below shows the exterior of the theater where *Fidelio* was performed in November 1805.

abated. Beethoven could even be observed singing as he played the piano, and he accepted an opportunity to perform in public.

"There Is Only One Beethoven"

One evening in October 1806, when Beethoven was staying at Prince Lichnowsky's castle in Ostrava, his host promised his French guests the chance to hear the composer play piano. But Beethoven disappeared. He did not want to perform—above all, not before officers in Napoleon's army. The prince insisted. Beethoven became angry and fled the castle on foot, in the pouring rain.

He spent the night in a neighboring village. The next day, before returning to Vienna, he wrote Lichnowsky: "Prince! What you are, you are by chance and by birth. What I am, I am by myself. There have been, there will be, thousands of princes. There is only one Beethoven."

Unhappily for Beethoven, however, there were few princes like Lichnowsky. The dispute that fall caused a total break. For the composer, it meant the loss of his 600 florins yearly and, even more serious, of his most reliable friend, whose devotion had never faltered in any circumstance.

Ferdinand Ries gave Franz Wegeler a description of the stormy quarrel between Beethoven and Prince Lichnowsky (opposite) in a letter of 28 December 1837: "Beethoven had grabbed a chair and was going to break it over the head of the prince—who had broken down the door of the room where Beethoven had locked himself in. Happily, Oppersdorf threw himself between them."

Beethoven now had several reasons to worry about his financial situation. The lukewarm reception given his last works by the Viennese public dampened any hopes of replacing Lichnowsky's stipend by presenting more concerts. Furthermore, the first performance of his Violin Concerto in D Major on 23 December was not wholly successful.

CHAPTER IV
TOWARD VICTORY

"Thus I can only seek support in the deepest, the most intimate part of myself; as for the external world, there is absolutely nothing there for me. No, nothing but injuries for me in friendship and feelings of the same genre."
Beethoven, May 1810

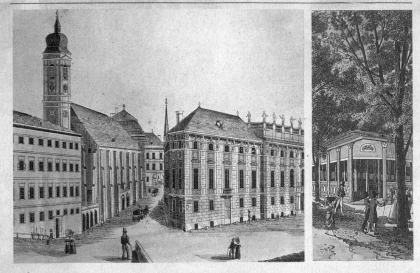

Preceding pages: *Lobkowitz Square in Vienna, c. 1760* and *Beethoven.* Baden (above right and below), a small spa about twenty miles from Vienna, was one of Beethoven's favorite vacation spots.

At the beginning of 1807 Prince Joseph Lobkowitz tried to meet Beethoven's most pressing financial needs by organizing two concerts in his palace devoted exclusively to the composer's music. The *Coriolan* Overture, newly completed, was performed, as were a piano concerto, several pages from *Fidelio*, and the four symphonies. The overture was the clear favorite.

Paralyzed since childhood, Prince Joseph Lobkowitz cultivated the arts and music. He maintained an orchestra in his palace (opposite above left).

Beethoven intended to garner additional revenues by bringing out some of his works in the major music publishing centers of Europe. He already had a strong relationship with the Bureau des arts et d'industrie in Vienna and with Breitkopf & Härtel in Leipzig. While negotiations with Pleyel in Paris fell through, he had a windfall in terms of London. Publisher and pianist-composer Muzio Clementi was passing through Vienna in the early spring of 1807. Beethoven gave him a warm reception.

Clementi's Shrewd Business Deal

Clementi wasted no time in taking advantage of the situation. According

to a letter he wrote to his partner F. W. Collard on 22 April 1807, after having duly praised certain of his colleague's works, he asked Beethoven if he had a London publisher.

" 'No,' says he.

'Suppose then that you prefer *me?*'

'With all my heart.'

'Done. What have you ready?'

'I'll bring you a list.' "

Beethoven returned with all his recent manuscripts under his arm. From the batch, Clementi chose a symphony, the *Coriolan* Overture, the Violin Concerto, the Piano Concerto no. 3, and the three *Razumovsky* Quartets. For some 2000 florins, he acquired the exclusive rights in all territories governed by the British Crown for these works along with the assurance that he would receive an arrangement of the Violin Concerto for piano and orchestra.

As was his habit, Beethoven was to spend the summer in villages outside Vienna, in Baden and Heiligenstadt. There, he worked on his next two symphonies and on a mass that Prince Nikolaus Esterházy, Haydn's patron, had commissioned for his wife's name day on 13 September. It was the first time Beethoven had broached the church repertoire. Unfortunately, the result satisfied neither the prince nor his guests, who could not look beyond Beethoven's awkwardness with the form to the mastery of the music.

Beethoven Submits an Application

Esterházy had just become one of a group of noblemen overseeing the theaters of the court. Prince Lobkowitz, also a member of this elite, suggested that Beethoven apply for a permanent post with the opera.

He did, in typical style: "The undersigned, having

Beethoven, unlike Mozart, held the pianist, composer, and pedagogue Muzio Clementi (above) in high esteem. He owned all his sonatas, around a hundred, and freely recommended them for his nephew's musical education.

In 1808 Beethoven wrote, "How happy I am as soon as I can wander in the woods, in the forests, among the trees, the rocks! No man could love the countryside as much as I." He is depicted opposite in his favorite setting, composing the *Pastoral* Symphony. Below, the manuscript of the Symphony no. 4.

"Prince Esterházy's wife spent her life seeking to console him of his happiness, and he himself overlooked nothing in the effort to amuse himself," reported the Baroness de Montet. In 1807 Esterházy (below; his palace is pictured at right and his château opposite) commissioned a mass for the princess' name day from Beethoven. It did not succeed in pleasing her. Beethoven ended up dedicating the 1812 edition to Prince Kinsky.

always taken as guide in his career not the mere wish to gain a livelihood but rather interest in art, the ennoblement of taste, and the elevation of his genius toward the highest ideal and perfection, has had to sacrifice his material gain and interests to the advantage of the Muse."

He continued in this vein, pointing out that his renown in foreign lands might well have led him to leave Vienna, but that he regarded that city as "the most deserving of any of his esteem and his devotion." Finally, he submitted two propositions:

"1. He commits and engages himself to compose at least one grand opera each year.... In exchange, he requests a fixed annual salary of two thousand four hundred florins as well as the gross receipts from the third performance of each of his operas.

"2. He commits himself to deliver each year and for free a small operetta or a *divertissement*, choral pieces, 'occasional' music, provided that he can stage each year an annual concert for his own benefit in one of the theaters."

Not surprisingly, he received no response. This time, Beethoven thought about leaving the Hapsburg capital for good. He spent the winter finishing the Sonata in A Major for Piano and Cello, op. 69, and, above all, the Symphony no. 5 in C Minor.

Shortly afterward, under the skies of Heiligenstadt, he also finished the Symphony no. 6 in F Major, the *Pastoral*. Returning to Vienna, he composed an additional Two Piano Trios, op. 70, and Fantasy for Piano, Orchestra, and Chorus, op. 80. The three symphonic works of that year, as well as the Piano Concerto no. 4 in G Major, extracts from the Mass in C Major, and the Fantasy for Piano, Orchestra, and Chorus were listed in the program of a grand concert that he gave for his own benefit on 22 December 1808.

Need He Leave Vienna?

In his mind he bade farewell to Vienna: Jérôme Bonaparte, Napoleon's brother, then ruling part of Germany, had just offered him a high salary to be Kapellmeister at his royal court in Kassel. But Beethoven

"As it is proven...that man cannot entirely devote himself to his art except in the condition of being free from all material care, and that it is only in this way that he can produce those great and elevated works that are the glory of art, the undersigned are resolved to shelter Mr. Ludwig van Beethoven from need."

Princes' decree
1 March 1809

had second thoughts: Did he really want to trade the spotlight of Europe's music capital for the shadows of Kassel? Would it not be better to arouse a reaction to keep him in Vienna?

Happily for Beethoven, he was never to depart to compose drum marches or use his feeble diplomatic skills to battle the singers, musicians, and French-style bureaucracy of Kassel. His Viennese admirers, led by Countess Marie Erdödy and Count Ignaz von Gleichenstein, launched an appeal to the aristocracy to assure that the musical genius not leave them and that the means be found to permit him to devote himself exclusively to his art.

Three dignitaries of the empire responded: jointly, they would provide Beethoven an annual stipend of 4000 florins for the rest of his life. Prince Lobkowitz committed himself to 700 florins; his father-in-law, Prince Kinsky,

"Provided that the lords consider themselves the coauthors of each new major work; such would be the point of view that I would most desire, considering the situation, and thus would the appearance be avoided according to which I am drawing on a pension for doing nothing."

Beethoven to Count
Ignaz von Gleichenstein
1809

UNSTERBLICHEN Goethe

hochachtungsvoll gewidmet

von

LUDWIG van BEETHOVEN,

112tes Werk.

Beethoven dedicated the cantata "Meeresstille und Glückliche Fahrt" (title page, left) to Goethe, who wrote the text.

to 1800; and the Archduke Rudolph of Hapsburg, who for some time had been studying piano and composition with Beethoven, to 1500. In exchange the composer had only to promise not to leave Vienna. Without being rich, Beethoven would never again be short of money.

Two months later, Napoleon's troops reached Vienna's city walls. The imperial family fled on 4 May, leaving sixteen thousand soldiers in place to defend the area. The day of his departure, Archduke Rudolph gave

At the moment when Austria and France were once again at war, Beethoven was working on the first movement of his Fifth Piano Concerto. Full of bellicose exaltation, he noted in the margin of his sketches, "Song of triumph for combat! Attack! Victory!" The arrival of Napoleon at Schönbrunn Castle in Vienna is pictured below.

Beethoven a melodic phrase of three notes (G, F, E-flat), based on which the composer wrote the Piano Sonata in E-flat Major, op. 81a *(Les Adieux)*, which told the "story" of the farewell, absence, and return of the archduke.

In Wartime, the Muses Fall Silent

French cannons opened fire on Vienna on 11 May. Beethoven took refuge in his brother's cellar and protected his ears from the noise of the bombardment by covering his head with pillows. It took him three months to regain his enthusiasm for work. But by the end of the year, he had relocated his inner resources and finished his Piano Concerto no. 5 in E-flat Major (the *Emperor*), the String Quartet in E-flat Major, op. 74 (the *Harp*), the Piano Fantasia in G Minor, op. 77 —which contemporaries described as reminiscent of Beethoven's improvisations on the piano—and, finally, the Piano Sonata in F-sharp Major, op. 78.

Peace was restored just as Beethoven was fervently writing theater music for Goethe's tragedy *Egmont*. But his difficulties had only begun. Austrian currency had been devalued. Beethoven succeeded less and less well in managing his worldly affairs. His solitude depressed him. He wrote only one work that year, the String Quartet in F Minor, op. 95, and another in 1811, the Piano Trio in B-flat Major, op. 97 (the *Archduke*). In September 1811 the emperor was obliged to put Prince Lobkowitz under financial guardianship. His guardians refused to honor the agreement the prince had signed for Beethoven's yearly stipend. Until 1815, when a court found in the composer's favor, he had to do without Lobkowitz's 700 florins. In 1812 Prince Kinsky died after a fall from a horse. Beethoven had to appear in court to demand his rights from the prince's estate. Meanwhile, holidays in Bohemian spas, plans for a reconciliation with Karl Lichnowsky, encounters with several young, pretty women with whom he became infatuated—nothing helped. Beethoven was perennially angry with Vienna and became increasingly gloomy.

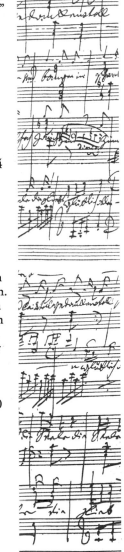

Beethoven's manuscript of the *Egmont*.

"Mistakes, Always Mistakes!"

During the years 1810 and 1811 publishers devoted more enthusiasm than ever to the publication of Beethoven's works. Never again would this activity reach such a level during his lifetime. While he did not do much composing, he spent a great deal of time reviewing printer's proofs. He became absorbed in making corrections: "Mistakes, always mistakes," he wrote to Härtel, his Leipzig publisher. "You are yourself a unique mistake.... Make mistakes as often as you want, make as many as you want, I will always respect you as much. Because it is the custom among men to respect others as long as they make no mistakes greater than they are themselves."

The end of 1811 and early 1812 were nearly entirely devoted to composing the Symphony no. 7 in A Major, which Beethoven finished on 13 May.

"One ought every day to listen to a little song, read a beautiful poem, see a worthwhile painting, and, if possible, say a few sensible words," wrote Goethe (above) in *Wilhelm Meister: The Years of Apprenticeship*.

A *Group of Listeners During the First Performance of the Seventh Symphony in Paris*

Encounters at the Spa

His health did not improve. He was forced to spend the entire summer "taking the waters" as he worked on the Symphony no. 8 in F Major. His first stop, Teplitz (now Teplice), was a fashionable spa where the best society converged, including Goethe. "I made the acquaintance of Beethoven at Teplitz," he wrote in 1812. "His talent overwhelms me with admiration. But he is unfortunately an unruly personality, who is certainly not wrong in finding the world detestable, but who, nonetheless, does not make it any more pleasant either for himself or for anyone else. He is easily excused, and he is to be pitied, for his hearing deserts him; this is perhaps less harmful from a musical than a social viewpoint. He who is already laconic by nature becomes doubly so through this infirmity."

During his stay at Teplice Beethoven drafted a fiery letter to the woman he christened his "Immortal Beloved." No one knows the true name of the recipient. Opinion wavers between the writer Bettina Brentano, her sister-in-law Antonie, and Josephine von Brunsvik. Antonie was definitely at the destination Beethoven indicated in the letter and they had been linked for a long time by a solid affection. As for Bettina, she was engaged in December 1810 to poet Achim von Arnim. Josephine, who had remarried two years earlier, had just been abandoned by her husband and was traveling alone, but the exact details of her route are unknown. Nine months later, she gave birth to a little girl. Could she have given way to that "physical love" that she had rejected seven years earlier? Returning finally to Vienna in November, but feeling fit, Beethoven composed his last Sonata for Piano and Violin, op. 96. It was performed on 19 December by Archduke Rudolph and French violinist Pierre Rode.

"Dear Bettina, cherished young girl," Beethoven wrote her (below). Was she the recipient of the letter to the Immortal Beloved (above)?

Economic and political difficulties no longer permitted productions of major symphonic concerts. Beethoven's depression was deep and tenacious, to the point that he wrote nothing more until summer.

War, Also, Can Be Put to Use

Suddenly, in June 1813, news arrived of Wellington's victory against the French forces at Vitoria, Spain. The anti-French coalition regained momentum. Popular enthusiasm for Wellington approached delirium.

J. N. Maelzel, who had made ear trumpets for Beethoven and had just invented the panharmonicon, a kind of mechanical orchestra (he later invented the metronome), commissioned the composer to write a piece for it on the Battle of Vitoria. It is difficult to imagine a more naive musical scenario than the one created for this curious symphony: Each army takes its position for attack, the English with their "Rule, Britannia," the French with the song "Marlborough s'en va-t'en-guerre." For the battle itself, the score even indicates musket fire.

After years of fighting the French (below: *Battle Between the Austrians and the French Near Vienna,* 1805), Wellington's first victory, 21 June 1813, aroused an enthusiastic reaction, comparable to that which followed Admiral Nelson's victory at Abukir fifteen years earlier. "I must show the English what blessings reside in their 'God Save the King,'" noted Beethoven. The end of his *Wellington's Victory* contains a fugal treatment of the British anthem.

Shortly afterward, Beethoven added a *Triumphal Symphony* to this movement and had the whole thing played in concert on 8 December 1813, along with the Seventh Symphony. Never before had he experienced such a triumph, and never would he know its equal. *Wellington's Victory* was performed again on 12 December and three more times at the beginning of 1814.

This piece of program music earned him a great deal of money and assured him public favor. But Beethoven was disconsolate that the Viennese had not at the outset valued his symphonies and other major works and instead favored a musical oddity whose bad taste he was already beginning to regret.

Fidelio Rescued from Oblivion

However, the success of *Wellington's Victory* at least gave rise to the opportunity to present a new performance of *Fidelio*. Beethoven hastened to rework the score from top to bottom for this revival, which took place on 23 May 1814 at the Kärntnertor theater. Its success equaled its earlier failure.

Although his deafness continued to gain ground, Beethoven seemed to open up again to the outside world. He regained his taste for life and work. On 16 August he finished the Piano Sonata in E Minor, op. 90.

The speed of his output accelerated, but he had to devote the greatest part of his time to occasional works and commissions of secondary interest.

"Resignation, the most profound resignation to your destiny....O God! Give me the strength to overcome myself!" wrote Beethoven in 1812. His ear trumpet rests on his manuscripts of the Ninth and *Eroica* symphonies, opposite; above, the String Trio in E-flat Major, op. 3.

In 1815 Europe caught its breath and licked its wounds. In the euphoria of the Congress of Vienna, Beethoven's music was applauded and honored. However, for Beethoven the outlook had already begun to darken: Lichnowsky and several other of Beethoven's supporters had died; others had left Vienna. Prince Razumovsky's palace, where his music had reigned supreme, had gone up in flames.

CHAPTER V
HEARTACHES

"The sounds living in his mind were no more than memories, specters of dead sounds, and his later works had on their forehead a stamp of death that makes one shiver."
Heinrich Heine
Lutetia, 1841

His morose mood had returned, his output declined. That year brought forth only one major effort, the Two Sonatas for Piano and Cello, op. 102.

Beethoven felt resolutely alone. His favorite brother, Caspar Carl, who also lived in Vienna, had fallen gravely ill. On 14 November he designated in his will that his wife, Johanna, and Ludwig be made coguardians of his only son, Karl. The child was only nine. Beethoven, who detested his sister-in-law, insisted he be made sole guardian, but Caspar Carl added a codicil to the will: "I by no means desire that my son be taken away from his mother, but that he stay with her as long as his future career permits; consequently, guardianship should be exercised equally by my wife and my brother." The next day, he died.

"Look upon Karl as your own child."
Beethoven, 1816

Beethoven called his youngest brother, Johann, "my non-fraternal brother."

Beethoven Hoped to Relieve His Solitude by Assuming the Role of Father

Despite the codicil, he wanted the child. In February 1816 he obtained a court judgment in his favor and placed Karl in a private school.

A judicial battle was launched over guardianship. It would last until 1820. During this struggle Beethoven proved fierce and pitiless. The affair absorbed his attention to such a degree that he could barely work.

At first he managed to finish the song cycle *To the Distant Beloved*, op. 98, and the Piano Sonata in A Major, op. 101. And there was no lack of projects...but nothing came of them. No work of any significance was to appear before 1819.

To bring his nephew home, Beethoven sought to put some order into his life. "What is a boarding school," he wrote on 13 May 1816, "compared to the attentive solicitude of a father for his child?"—because he now regarded himself as Karl's father.

Beginning in March, he began feeling poorly. He sought to dispel his loneliness

Preceding pages: *Beethoven Composing* and bound Beethoven manuscripts owned by Archduke Rudolph with a metronome by J. N. Maelzel.

by reading Plutarch, Shakespeare, or Schiller, quotations from whom are sprinkled throughout his notes. After nearly a year in this state, on 9 September 1817 he remarked, "Without music, every day I feel closer to the grave."

In November, after having nurtured himself on the fugues of J. S. Bach, he wrote the Fugue in D Major for string quintet, op. 137, at the request of his friend Tobias Haslinger.

A Mother Is Always a Mother

He never gave up the idea of bringing Karl home with him. As he was feeling better in general, he took the boy out of Giannatasio del Rio's school in January 1818. He hired a private tutor to give him lessons; it was out of the question that Karl should leave home to go to school, for fear that his mother would take advantage of the fact to establish secret contact. But Johanna knew how to take advantage of Beethoven's servants, who

Beethoven preferred certain musical forms—the sonata, the symphony, chamber music, and, in particular, the string quartet—to the detriment of others, such as vocal music. In this regard, the song cycle *To the Distant Beloved* (title page, above) was a relative rarity. The year of its composition, 1816, was haunted by unhappiness: "We…are born only for suffering and for joy," he wrote to the Countess Marie Erdödy, "and one can almost say that the loftiest seize joy across suffering."

always had a complaint against their master. Soon, Karl was visiting his mother. The crime discovered, he was treated roughly by his uncle. He exposed the role played by the servants, who were sent away on the spot. "Karl has acted badly," Beethoven concluded, "but a mother, even a bad mother, is always a mother."

At the end of May uncle and nephew moved to Mödling, a little village south of Vienna, to spend the summer months. The child attended the school run by Father Fröhlich, but his attitude was so rebellious that Beethoven was forced to take him home at the end of a month. He hired a tutor for a trimester to prepare Karl to enter Vienna's academic gymnasium, the secondary school.

The situation became more complicated when the child ran away to his mother's. The courtroom battle recommenced. Finally, thanks to pressure from well-placed friends, the uncle gained guardianship, in April 1820. The humiliations and depressions the affair caused had prevented Beethoven from devoting himself to his work. But his style had ripened in silence.

A New Beethoven

At the same time he was writing the Fugue for string quintet, op. 137, he sketched out the Piano Sonata in B-flat Major, op. 106 (the *Hammerklavier*), but he was unable to finish it until spring 1819. It begins in typical Beethoven fashion: an assertive, imperious, *fortissimo* gesture, indicating neither rhythm nor melody. Rather, it is a hammering on a single chord that, at the last moment, it seems, sinks down a third. The same gesture is repeated

"Beethoven's outward appearance had something unusual and striking about it.... Generally lost in thought and humming to himself, he frequently gesticulated with his arms while walking," Stephan von Breuning, Beethoven's friend from Bonn, recalled. Below, *The Solitary Master*. Opposite, the village of Mödling.

immediately in the treble. This introduction has the appearance of an epigraph. It is followed by the true theme, played *piano*—responding to the D–B-flat that concluded the opening, it starts by ascending the same third, from B-flat to D. At the end, the same thirds are played descending, just as in the epigraph.

The initial gesture of the Sonata in B-flat Major acts like a generative cell. The germ of the work, it presents a major third that, in turn, determines all the developments to come. Even the theme of the immense final fugue is based on it. This process was certainly not new to Beethoven; it appeared in the four initial notes of the Fifth Symphony, another gesture that engenders an entire work! But Beethoven here demanded more rigor of himself than ever before: Starting from this single initiating motif, he worked out the rest of the piece as if it were a logical construction. This developmental model had been propounded by Baron d'Holbach, a French philosopher of the Enlightenment, in his book *The System of Nature*, published in Paris the year Beethoven was born. Mozart had been the first to integrate this model into his work, rejecting the notion, later identified with the Romantic school of Sturm und Drang, that the collision of ideas foreign to one another, even if themselves basically straightforward, was enough to give both strength and unity to a piece.

Essentially, then, the procedure Beethoven used is contrary to the Romantic style. Educated in the climate of the Enlightenment, he remained a Classical spirit. This does not, however, diminish his deep originality, characterized above all by the dominant place he accorded to rhythm. Beethoven's rhythmic movement

Baron d'Holbach was one of the key figures of the Enlightenment; he contributed hundreds of articles to Denis Diderot's famous *Encyclopedia*.

"To write true church music," Beethoven noted in 1818, "survey the old chorales of the monks, etc." In fact, his *Missa Solemnis* bore witness to an ongoing concern with linking the liturgical word and material from ancient chant. (Beethoven's sketches for it are shown below and opposite.)

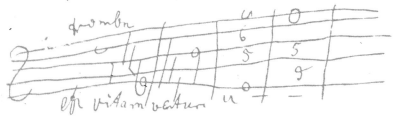

propels the work forward, often obstinately, almost against its will. It speaks to the most elementary drives in the individual; it betrays the violent, impulsive temperament of the composer. Virtuosity is entirely put at its disposal, as well as all the means possible to generate contrast.

Beethoven Works on a Second Mass

He wanted to create a monumental work in honor of his pupil, protector, and friend Archduke Rudolph. The young Hapsburg was to be appointed to the archbishop's seat of Olomouc in Moravia on 19 March 1820. But his domestic problems prevented Beethoven from finishing the work in the time allotted; by the date of the ceremony, only the Kyrie and the Gloria were written.

It took him another three years to complete work on the *Missa Solemnis.* What it had lost in not being timely, it gained in becoming the religious testament of its author.

He weighed each word of the piece, insistent on the mystery of faith— and on the word *credo* ("I believe")—passing more rapidly over other liturgical articles of the dogma; nature and liberty remained his ruling ideas.

In place of finishing his mass immediately, Beethoven wrote three piano sonatas in rapid succession. The last note of opus 109, the E major, was put on paper in autumn 1820; that of opus 110, the A-flat major, on 25 December 1821; and that of opus 111, the C minor, the following 13 January. Having said everything he could in the sonata form, he turned back to other instrumental genres; the piano, instrument of intimacy, had helped him out of the rut into which he had fallen. It carried him to a new surge of creativity that was to culminate not only in the finished *Missa Solemnis* but also in the *Diabelli* Variations (1823), the Symphony no. 9 in D Minor (1824), and the last six string quartets (1825–6).

"The sight of one of Beethoven's first sketches with its wild impatient strokes, its chaotic mixture of motifs begun and discarded, and with the creative fury, the superabundance of his genius, compressed into a few pencil strokes is physically exciting to me because it is mentally exciting."

Stefan Zweig
The World of Yesterday
1943

Spring 1822 brought Gioacchino Rossini, composer of brilliant Italian operas, to the banks of the Danube. Evening after evening, the public was enraptured. The difficulties Viennese theaters had experienced following the wars with the French were forgotten. Even Beethoven took a liking to the composer's whimsical *Barber of Seville,* whose score he had brought to him before attending a performance. In one stroke, the climate for opera was reestablished; already, a revival of *Fidelio* was being prepared. Was life finally beginning to assume an orderly direction?

"When Beethoven's soul soars over this sacred choir, what fervent prayer rises toward God!"
George Sand
Lettres d'un voyageur

CHAPTER VI
SONG OF
HUMANITY

Ludwig Van Beethoven

Beethoven decided to conduct at least the general rehearsal of his opera. For the overture, the orchestral musicians arranged themselves as well as they could to make up for the somewhat vague directions of their deaf conductor. But catastrophe struck at the beginning of the first act: The orchestra and the singers could not manage to play together. They tried to start again, but to no avail. Finally, Beethoven understood what was going on; he precipitously returned home and covered his face with his hands.

Unexpected Success: A New Beginning

However, on the evening of 3 November 1822, *Fidelio* transported the public with enthusiasm. The young Wilhelmine Schröder was admirable in the role of Leonore. The opera was held over for several weeks. Beethoven thought of returning to the lyric-theater genre, but first he wanted to finish up projects already underway. He spent a good part of the year on a new string quartet and on the Symphony no. 9 in D Minor, which the London Philharmonic Society had been awaiting for a long time.

In mid-November he received a letter that confirmed his desire to write for string quartet: "As passionate a music lover as I am a great admirer of your talent," the author wrote, "I take the liberty of writing you to ask if you would not consent to compose one, two, or three new string quartets, for which I would have the pleasure of paying you for whatever trouble you judge it appropriate to denote."

The writer indicated that he himself played the cello. It was none other than the young Russian prince Nikolai Galitzin. His request paralleled Beethoven's own intentions so exactly that it was doubly sure to be

P receding pages: *Beethoven Composing the "Missa Solemnis"* and his signature on the manuscript title page of the Ninth Symphony; a page from the score is shown above.

R ight: *Performance of "Fidelio" on 28 January 1868*

fulfilled. But for the time being, Beethoven concentrated on finishing the Ninth Symphony.

The work engrossed him until February 1824, as he changed his mind several times about its conclusion. At the beginning of summer 1823 he was still thinking about an instrumental finale using a theme that, in the end, was to serve for the last movement of the String Quartet in A Minor, op. 132.

Wilhelmine Schröder as *Fidelio*'s Leonore.

A Choral Apotheosis

Soon afterward he arrived at a completely different
solution: He would set Friedrich Schiller's 1785 poem
"Ode to Joy" to music. The idea was an old one, but
until this point he had been saving it for another
composition. In writing this poem Schiller had
been inspired by collections of Freemason poetry,
and he adopted their format of alternation between a
soloist and a choral response. While neither Schiller
nor Beethoven were Freemasons, both shared the
masonic ideal of universal fraternization.

Rumor spread in Vienna that the new
symphony was finally completed. The only
problem was that Beethoven had promised
the first production to the London
Philharmonic Society, or worse, to the king
of Prussia. Viennese pride was sufficiently
wounded that thirty "art lovers," old friends
and old enemies combined, sent him a petition:
"We know that the crown of your great
symphonies has recently had the addition of an
immortal flower. For years already, since the
thundering of the Battle of Vitoria died away, we
have waited and we have hoped. Open anew the
treasure of your inspiration and lavish it on us as
you have before! Do not disappoint any longer the
public who awaits!"

Despite the commitments to London and last-
minute difficulties, the concert was announced for
7 May 1824, in the Kärntnertor theater. Two
rehearsals only. Empty seats. Not one member of
the imperial family. A faltering beginning—after
three excerpts from the *Missa Solemnis*, some
audience members left. Then, suddenly: Triumph!
The irresistible ascension of the Ninth Symphony
toward the "Ode to Joy" infused the entire hall with
exaltation and jubilation.

But receipts from the evening were
disappointing, as they were for the next
performance, on 23 May. Beethoven was
discouraged. More than ever, he turned to

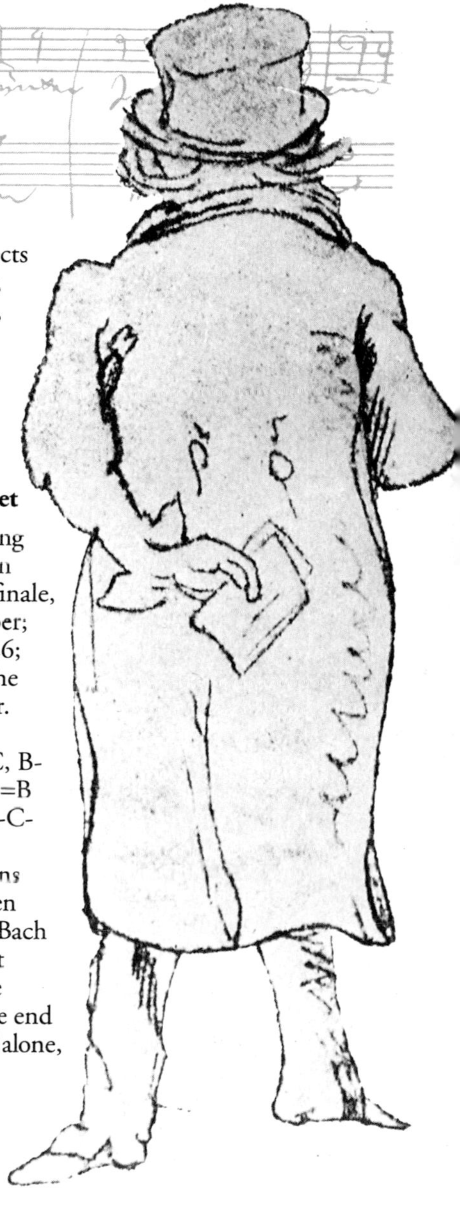

chamber music. He put aside his projects for a new opera and a tenth symphony, on which he was still working in 1824, and at last he completed, in February 1825, the String Quartet in E-flat Major, op. 127, begun in May 1822 but abandoned in favor of the Ninth Symphony.

Ultimate Return to the String Quartet

In succession, Beethoven wrote the string quartets in A minor, op. 132, in July; in B-flat major, op. 130, and its original finale, the Grosse Fugue, op. 133, in November; in C-sharp minor, op. 131, in July 1826; in F major, op. 135, in October; and the new finale for opus 130 that November.

Throughout these works, Beethoven slipped in the thematic cell B-flat, A, C, B-natural. (In the German system, B-flat=B and B-natural=H; thus, this spells B-A-C-H.) He pushed melody and harmony, making use of counterpoint, into regions where not even he himself had ever been —and where he had only Mozart and Bach as companions. Here, he imposed strict structures on his imagination; there, he allowed himself complete liberty. In the end he created a world that existed by itself alone,

A sketch from the "Ode to Joy" is shown above; the drawings of Beethoven on both pages were made by von Boehm.

that lived by the power of its authority, with reference to nothing else, not even the Ninth Symphony or the *Missa Solemnis*.

As he composed the quartets, his problems with Karl grew worse. His nephew failed at everything he undertook—he even botched his own suicide, on 29 July 1826. Beethoven reluctantly agreed that Karl should join the military. While waiting for his departure to join his regiment, uncle and nephew spent several weeks in Gneixendorf, the home of Beethoven's brother Johann. At the beginning of December Beethoven returned to Vienna, on the back of an open milk cart in a blinding rain. He contracted pneumonia, soon complicated by jaundice.

From this point on, Beethoven was confined to his deathbed. He now had only the joy of reading, of visitors, and of music that he could see being played in his room without being able to hear it.

"Sing, Sing Then!"

One of his last visitors, the tenor Luigi Cramolini, came to introduce him to his fiancée. "When we entered," Cramolini recounted, "the poor man was lying in bed, oppressed with dropsy. From his large eyes open and sparkling, he watched me. Then he held out his left hand and smiled: 'Well, here's the little Luigi, and now he's engaged…. You make a handsome couple. And from what I can read, you are also a couple of gallant artists.'

"He held out paper and pencil to us and the conversation proceeded through writing, while he spoke sometimes, in an almost incomprehensible fashion. Then he asked us to sing something for him. Schindler sat down at one of the grand pianos located side by side in the center of the room, and we placed ourselves in front of Beethoven. I wrote that I was going to sing his

Mementos: soup-spoon and ladle, ear trumpet, medal of Louis XVIII, a conductor's baton and cane.

"It seems to me that I've barely written a few notes," Beethoven wrote to the publisher Schott on 17 September 1824. It is likely that his music was played at *A Musical Evening in the Home of Bettina von Arnim in Berlin,* above. Bettina Brentano was a close friend of both Beethoven and Goethe.

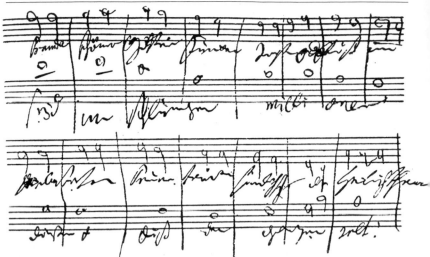

'Adelaide,' a piece with which I had become well known in the artistic world. Beethoven agreed with a friendly gesture. But when I was about to start, my throat tightened so with emotion that I was absolutely incapable of singing. I requested Schindler to wait a moment while I regained my composure. Beethoven asked what had happened, why I wasn't singing, and, when Schindler told him the reason, he laughed heartily and said to me:

" 'Sing, sing then, my dear Luigi; unfortunately I can't hear you, but I would like at least to see you sing.'

Sketch for the "Ode to Joy."

Did Schubert and Beethoven ever meet, as the title of the engraving below would have us believe? Schubert appears to have consistently sought to speak with the older composer, frequenting the cafés where he knew he might meet him, but his timid disposition prevented him from actually addressing Beethoven.

The drawing of *Beethoven on His Deathbed* (opposite above) is dated 28 March, two days after he died. The funeral (opposite below) took place on 29 March.

"Finally, I regained my forces and sang with enthusiasm the song of all songs, the divine 'Adelaide' of Beethoven. When I had finished, he called me to his bed and said, tightly squeezing my hand:

" 'I saw from your breathing that you sang it the way it should be, and I read on your face that you felt what you sang. You have given me great pleasure.'

"I was suffused with happiness on hearing this great man's appraisal, and I wiped away a tear. When I tried to kiss his hands, he hastily withdrew them, saying:

" 'Save that for your dear mama!' "

Shortly afterward, on 26 March 1827, Beethoven died. Heartless Vienna bestowed on the dead composer all the honors it had refused him during his life. "Never had an emperor a funeral to equal it," wrote Therese von Brunsvik. "Thirty thousand people accompanied him to the gravesite." They would have done equally well to listen to his music.

"Beethoven opened his eyes wide; he raised his right hand and, fist clenched, his expression ferocious and menacing, he fixed his gaze upward for several seconds....
When his hand fell back on the bed, his eyes were half shut."

Anselm Hüttenbrenner

DOCUMENTS

Wild and solitary, tragic hero and impetuous genius,
a lost romantic questing for the Absolute:
This is how Beethoven appeared to his contemporaries,
and so he remains for all of us.

Beethoven's Daily Life

In the eyes of those who saw him live, create, and perform music, Beethoven seemed like a "wild man"—an uncouth savage. This impression increased as deafness enveloped him, and those around him were constantly working to forestall the difficulties that arose from his deafness.

The "Wild Man" of the Salons

Beethoven is the most celebrated of the living composers in Vienna and, in certain departments, the foremost of his day. Though not an old man, he is lost to society in consequence of his extreme deafness, which has rendered him almost unsocial. The neglect of his person which he exhibits gives him a somewhat wild appearance. His features are strong and prominent; his eye is full of rude energy; his hair, which neither comb nor scissors seem to have visited for years, overshadows his broad brow in a quantity and confusion to which only the snakes round a Gorgon's head offer a parallel.

His general behaviour does not ill accord with the unpromising exterior. Except when he is among his chosen friends, kindliness or affability are not his characteristics. The total loss of hearing has deprived him of all the pleasure which society can give, and perhaps soured his temper. He used to frequent a particular cellar, where he spent the evening in a corner, beyond the reach of all the chattering and disputation of a public room, drinking wine and beer, eating cheese and red herrings, and studying the newspapers. One evening a person took a seat near him whose

countenance did not please him. He looked hard at the stranger, and spat on the floor as if he had seen a toad; then glanced at the newspaper, then again at the intruder, and spat again, his hair bristling gradually into more shaggy ferocity, till he closed the alternation of spitting and staring, by fairly exclaiming "What a scoundrelly phiz!" and rushing out of the room. Even among his oldest friends he must be humoured like a wayward child.

He has always a small paper book with him, and what conversation takes place is carried on in writing. In this, too, although it is not lined, he instantly jots down any musical idea which strikes him. These notes would be utterly unintelligible even to another musician, for they have thus no comparative value; he alone has in his own mind the thread by which he brings out of this labyrinth of dots and circles the richest and most astounding harmonies. The moment he is seated at the piano, he is evidently unconscious that there is anything in existence but himself and his instrument; and, considering how very deaf he is, it seems impossible that he should hear all he plays. Accordingly, when playing very *piano*, he often does not bring out a single note. He hears it himself in the "mind's ear." While his eye, and the almost imperceptible motion of his fingers, show that he is following out the strain in his own soul through all its dying gradations, the instrument is actually as dumb as the musician is deaf.

The seventeen-year-old Beethoven plays for Mozart.

Coaxing the "Wild Man" to Perform

I have heard him play; but to bring him so far required some management, so great is his horror of being anything like exhibited. Had he been plainly asked to do the company that favour, he would have flatly refused; he had to be cheated into it. Every person left the room,

except Beethoven and the master of the house, one of his most intimate acquaintances. These two carried on a conversation in the paper-book about bank stock. The gentleman, as if by chance, struck the keys of the open piano, beside which they were sitting, gradually began to run over one of Beethoven's own compositions, made a thousand errors, and speedily blundered one passage so thoroughly, that the composer condescended to stretch out his hand and put him right. It was enough; the hand was on the piano; his companion immediately left him, on some pretext, and joined the rest of the company, who in the next room, from which they could see and hear everything, were patiently waiting the issue of this tiresome conjuration. Beethoven, left alone, seated himself at the piano. At first he only struck now and then a few hurried and interrupted notes, as if afraid of being detected in a crime; but gradually he forgot everything else, and ran on during half an hour in a fantasy, in a style extremely varied, and marked, above all, by the most abrupt transitions. The amateurs were enraptured; to the uninitiated it was more interesting to observe how the music of the man's soul passed over his countenance. He seems to feel the bold, the commanding, and the impetuous, more than what is soothing or gentle. The muscles of the face swell, and its veins start out; the wild eye rolls doubly wild, the mouth quivers, and Beethoven looks like a wizard, overpowered by the demons whom he himself has called up.

John Russell
A Tour in Germany, and Some of the Southern Provinces of the Austrian Empire, in 1820, 1821, 1822
1828

BEETHOVEN improvisant chez le cordonnier Franz à Bonn. — (Composition de M. Lix.)

Use of Time

Beethoven rose at daybreak, no matter what the season, and went at once to his work-table. There he worked until two or three o'clock, when he took his midday meal. In the interim he usually ran out into the open two or three times, where he also "worked while walking." Such excursions seldom exceeded a full hour's time, and resembled the swarming out of the bee to gather honey. They never varied with the seasons and neither cold nor heat were noticed.

The afternoons were dedicated to regular promenades; and at a later hour Beethoven was wont to hunt up some favorite beer-house, in order to read the news of the day, if he had not already satisfied this need at some café. At the time when the English parliament was sitting, however, the *Allgemeine Zeitung* was regularly read at home for the sake of the debates. It will be easily understood that our politico was arrayed on the side of the Opposition. Nor was his great pre-dilection for Lord Brougham, Hume and other Opposition orators necessary to this end.

Beethoven always spent his winter evenings at home, and devoted them to serious reading. It was but seldom that one saw him busy with music-paper in the evening, since writing music was too taxing for his eyes. In former years this may not have been the case; yet it is quite certain that at no time did he employ the evening hours for composition (creation). At ten o'clock at the latest he went to bed.

Moments of Meditation

Washing and bathing were among the most indispensable necessities of existence for Beethoven. In this respect he was a thorough Oriental. Mohammed has by no means pre-scribed too many ablutions to suit him. If, while he was working, he did not go out during the forenoon, in order to compose himself, he would stand at the wash-basin, often in extremest negligée and pour great pitchersfull of water over his hands, at the same time howling or, for a change, growling out the whole gamut of the scale, ascending and descending; then, before long, he would pace the room, his eyes rolling or fixed in a stare, jot down a few notes and again return to his water pouring and howling.

These were moments of profoundest meditation, nothing worth making a great fuss about had they not resulted in disagreeable consequences in two directions. In the first place, they often incited his servants to laughter, observing which the Master would fly into a rage, which on occasion led him to yield to ridiculous outbreaks. Or he would get into a fight with the landlord when the water leaked through the floor which, unfortunately, often happened. This was a principal reason why Beethoven was everywhere unwelcome as a lodger.

Food and Drink

At breakfast Beethoven drank coffee, which he usually prepared himself in a percolator. Coffee seems to have been the nourishment with which he could least dispense and in his procedure with regard to its preparation he was as careful as the Orientals are known to be. Sixty beans to a cup was the allotment and the beans often were counted out exactly, especially when guests were present.

Among his favorite dishes was maccaroni with Parmesan cheese. Furthermore, all fish dishes were his special predilection. Hence guests usually were invited for Friday when a full-weight *Schill* (a Danube fish resembling the haddock) with potatoes could be served. Supper was hardly taken into account. A plate of soup and some remnants of the midday meal was all that he took. His favorite beverage was fresh spring water which, in summer, he drank in well-nigh inordinate quantities. Among wines he preferred the Hungarian, *Ofen* variety. Unfortunately he liked best the adulterated wines which did great damage to his weak intestines. But warnings were of no avail in this case. Our Master also liked to drink a good glass of beer in the evening, with which he smoked a pipeful of tobacco and kept the news-sheets company.

Beethoven still often visited taverns and coffee-houses in his last years, but insisted in coming in at a back door and being allowed to sit in a room apart. Strangers who wished to see him were directed thither; for he was not changeable and always chose a coffee-house near his own dwelling. He very seldom allowed himself to be drawn into conversation with strangers presented to him in these places. When he had run through the last news-sheet he would hurriedly depart again through the back door.

Anton Schindler
Life of Beethoven
1840

B*eethoven at the Piano*

Beethoven's Letters

Although as he became increasingly deaf the written word, in his "conversation books," became his sole means of communication with the external world, Beethoven rarely fully unburdened himself in his letters. He more easily spoke of mundane life or publishing matters than aesthetics or feelings. On the rare occasions when he wrote freely, the outpouring was more violent than his music.

The Heiligenstadt Testament

FOR MY BROTHERS CARL AND [JOHANN] BEETHOVEN

Oh you men who think or say that I am malevolent, stubborn, or misanthropic, how greatly do you wrong me. You do not know the secret cause which makes me seem that way to you. From childhood on, my heart and soul have been full of the tender feeling of goodwill, and I was ever inclined to accomplish great things. But, think that for six years now I

"Speak louder, shout, for I am deaf." Ah, how could I possibly admit an infirmity in the *one sense* which ought to be more perfect in me than in others, a sense which I once possessed in the highest perfection, a perfection such as few in my profession enjoy or ever have enjoyed.—Oh I cannot do it; therefore forgive me when you see me draw back when I would have gladly mingled with you. My misfortune is doubly painful to me because I am bound to be misunderstood; for me there can be no relaxation with my fellow men, no refined conversations, no mutual exchange of ideas. I must live almost alone, like one who has been banished; I can mix with society only as much as true necessity demands. If I approach near to people a hot terror seizes upon me, and I fear being exposed to the danger that my condition might be noticed. Thus it has been during the last six months which I have spent in the country. By ordering me to spare my hearing as much as possible, my intelligent doctor almost fell in with my own present frame of mind, though sometimes I ran counter to it by yielding to my desire for companionship. But what a humiliation for me when someone standing next to me heard a flute in the distance and *I heard nothing*, or someone heard a *shepherd singing* and again I heard nothing. Such incidents drove me almost to despair; a little more of that and I would have ended my life—it was only *my art* that held me back. Ah, it seemed to me impossible to leave the world until I had brought forth all that I felt was within me. So I endured this wretched existence—truly wretched for so susceptible a body, which can be thrown by a sudden change from the

have been hopelessly afflicted, made worse by senseless physicians, from year to year deceived with hopes of improvement, finally compelled to face the prospect of *a lasting malady* (whose cure will take years or, perhaps, be impossible). Though born with a fiery, active temperament, even susceptible to the diversions of society, I was soon compelled to withdraw myself, to live life alone. If at times I tried to forget all this, oh how harshly was I flung back by the doubly sad experience of my bad hearing. Yet it was impossible for me to say to people,

best condition to the very worst.—
Patience, they say, is what I must now
choose for my guide, and I have done
so—I hope my determination will
remain firm to endure until it pleases
the inexorable Parcae to break the
thread. Perhaps I shall get better,
perhaps not; I am ready.—Forced to
become a philosopher already in my
twenty-eighth year,—oh it is not
easy, and for the artist much more
difficult than for anyone else.—Divine
One, thou seest my inmost soul;
thou knowest that therein dwells the
love of mankind and the desire to do
good.—Oh fellow men, when at
some point you read this, consider then
that you have done me an injustice;
someone who has had misfortune may
console himself to find a similar case
to his, who despite all the limitations of
Nature nevertheless did everything
within his powers to become accepted
among worthy artists and men.—You,
my brothers Carl and [Johann], as soon
as I am dead, if Dr. Schmidt is still
alive, ask him in my name to describe
my malady, and attach this written
document to his account of my illness
so that so far as is possible at least the
world may become reconciled to me
after my death.—At the same time, I
declare you two to be the heirs to my
small fortune (if so it can be called);
divide it fairly; bear with and help
each other. What injury you have done
me you know was long ago forgiven.
To you, brother Carl, I give special
thanks for the attachment you have
shown me of late. It is my wish that you
may have a better and freer life than I
have had. Recommend *virtue* to your
children; it alone, not money, can
make them happy. I speak from
experience; this was what upheld me

in time of misery. Thanks to it and
to my art, I did not end my life by
suicide—Farewell and love each
other—I thank all my friends,
particularly *Prince Lichnowsky* and
Professor Schmidt—I would like
the instruments from Prince L. to be
preserved by one of you, but not to
be the cause of strife between you, and
as soon as they can serve you a better
purpose, then sell them. How happy I
shall be if I can still be helpful to you
in my grave—so be it.—With joy I
hasten to meet death.—If it comes
before I have had the chance to develop
all my artistic capacities, it will still
be coming too soon despite my harsh
fate, and I should probably wish it
later—yet even so I should be happy,
for would it not free me from a state of
endless suffering?—Come when thou
wilt, I shall meet thee bravely.—
Farewell and do not wholly forget me
when I am dead; I deserve this from
you, for during my lifetime I was
thinking of you often and of ways to
make you happy—please be so—

Ludwig van Beethoven
Heiglnstadt, [Heiligenstadt]
October 6th, 1802

FOR MY BROTHERS CARL AND
[JOHANN] TO BE READ AND
EXECUTED AFTER MY DEATH.

Heiglnstadt, October 10th, 1802
Thus I bid thee farewell—and indeed
sadly.—Yes, that fond hope—which I
brought here with me, to be cured to a
degree at least—this I must now wholly
abandon. As the leaves of autumn fall
and are withered—so likewise has my
hope been blighted—I leave here—
almost as I came—even the high
courage—which often inspired me in

the beautiful days of summer—has disappeared—Oh Providence—grant me at last but one day of *pure joy*—it is so long since real joy echoed in my heart—Oh when—Oh when, Oh Divine One—shall I feel it again in the temple of nature and of mankind— Never?—No—Oh that would be too hard.

From Maynard Solomon
Beethoven
1977

Letters to the Immortal Beloved

July 6, in the morning

My angel, my all, my very self—

Only a few words today and at that with pencil (with yours)— Not till tomorrow will my lodgings be definitely determined upon—what a useless waste of time— Why this deep sorrow when necessity speaks—can our love endure except through sacrifices, through not demanding everything from one another; can you change the fact that you are not wholly mine, I not wholly thine— Oh God, look out into the beauties of nature and comfort your heart with that which must be— Love demands everything and that very justly—*thus it is to me with you, and to you with me.* But you forget so easily that I must live *for me and for you;* if we were wholly united you would feel the pain of it as little as I—My journey was a fearful one; I did not reach here until 4 o'clock yesterday morning. Lacking horses the postcoach chose another route, but what an awful one; at the stage before the last I was warned not to travel at night; I was made fearful of

Beethoven's House in Heiligenstadt

a forest, but that only made me the more eager—and I was wrong. The coach must needs break down on the wretched road, a bottomless mud road. Without such postilions as I had with me I should have remained stuck in the road. Esterhazy, traveling the usual road here, had the same fate with eight horses that I had with four—Yet I got some pleasure out of it, as I always do when I successfully overcome difficulties—Now a quick change to things internal from things external. We shall surely see each other soon; moreover, today I cannot share with you the thoughts I have had during these last few days touching my own life— If our hearts were always close together, I would have none of these. My heart

is full of so many things to say to you— ah—there are moments when I feel that speech amounts to nothing at all— Cheer up—remain my true, my only treasure, my all as I am yours. The gods must send us the rest, what for us must and shall be—

Your faithful Ludwig

Evening, Monday, July 6
You are suffering, my dearest creature—only now have I learned that letters must be posted very early in the morning on Mondays— Thursdays—the only days on which the mail-coach goes from here to K.—You are suffering— Ah, wherever I am, there you are also— I will arrange it with you and me that I can live with you. What a life!!!! thus!!!! without you—pursued by the goodness of mankind hither and thither— which I as little want to deserve as I deserve it—Humility of man towards man—it pains me—and when I consider myself in relation to the universe, what am I and what is He—whom we call the greatest—and yet—herein lies the divine in man— I weep when I reflect that you will probably not receive the first report from me until Saturday— Much as you love me—I love you more— But do not ever conceal yourself from me— good night—As I am taking the baths I must go to bed— Oh God—so near! so far! Is not our love truly a heavenly structure, and also as firm as the vault of Heaven? —

Good morning, on July 7
Though still in bed, my thoughts go out to you, my Immortal Beloved, now and then joyfully, then sadly, waiting to learn whether or not fate will hear

The spirit of Sturm und Drang, as in this 1849 painting by Moritz von Schwind, permeates Beethoven's writings.

us—I can live only wholly with you or not at all— Yes, I am resolved to wander so long away from you until I can fly to your arms and say that I am really at home with you, and can send my soul enwrapped in you into the land of spirits— Yes, unhappily it must be so— You will be the more contained since you know my fidelity to you. No one else can ever possess my heart—never—never—Oh God, why must one be parted from one whom one so loves. And yet my life in V[ienna] is now a wretched life— Your love makes me at once the happiest and the unhappiest of men— At my age I need a steady, quiet life—can that be so in our connection? My angel, I have just been told that the mail-coach goes every day—therefore I must close at once so that you may receive the l[etter] at once.— Be calm, only by a calm consideration of our existence can we achieve our purpose to live together— Be calm—love me— today—yesterday—what tearful longings for you—you—you—my life—my all—farewell.— Oh continue to love me—never misjudge the most faithful heart of your beloved L.

ever thine
ever mine
ever ours

From Maynard Solomon
Beethoven
1977

Deafness Transfigured

Beethoven's deafness has often been used to explain his work. Do not the "oddities" of his orchestration prove he was unable to hear what he imagined? Did not his isolation from the world of sound develop his penchant for musical abstraction? Such clichés have endured since the 19th century. But true musicians have never been misled.

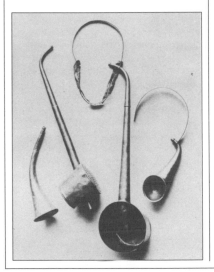

The more he thus lost connection with the outer world, the clearer was his inward vision. The surer he felt of his inner wealth, the more confidently did he make his demands outwards; and he actually required from his friends and patrons that they should no longer *pay* him for his works, but so provide for him that he might work for himself regardless of the world. And it actually came to pass, for the first time in the life of a musician, that a few well-disposed men of rank pledged themselves to keep Beethoven independent in the sense desired. Arrived at a similar turning-point in his life, Mozart perished, prematurely exhausted. But the great kindness conferred upon Beethoven, although he did not enjoy it long without interruption or diminution, nevertheless laid the foundation to the peculiar harmony, which was henceforth apparent in the master's life, no matter how strangely constituted. He felt himself victorious, and knew that he belonged to the world only as a free man. The world had to take him as he was. He treated his aristocratic benefactors despotically, and nothing could be got from him save what he felt disposed to give, and at his own time.

But he never felt inclined for anything save that which solely and continually occupied him: the magician's disport with the shapes of his inner world. For the outer world now became extinct to him; not that blindness robbed him of its view, but because *deafness* finally kept it at a distance from his hearing. The ear was the only organ through which the outer

Ear trumpets made by J. N. Maelzel for Beethoven.

world could still reach and disturb him; it had long since faded to his eye. What did the enraptured dreamer *see*, when, fixedly staring, with open eyes, he wandered through the crowded streets of Vienna, solely animated by the waking of his inner world of tones?

The beginning and increase of trouble in his ear pained him dreadfully, and induced profound melancholy, but after complete deafness had set in, no particular complaints were heard from him; none whatever about his incapacity to listen to musical performances; the intercourse of daily life only, which never had attracted him much, was rendered more difficult, and he now avoided it the more.

A musician without hearing! could a blind painter be imagined?

But we know of a blind *Seer*. Tiresias, to whom the phenomenal world was closed, but who, with inward vision, saw the basis of all phenomena,—and the deaf musician who listens to his inner harmonies undisturbed by the noise of life, who speaks from the depths to a world that has nothing more to say to him—now resembles the seer.

Thus genius, delivered from the impress of external things, exists wholly in and for itself. What wonders would have been disclosed to one who could have seen Beethoven with the vision of Tiresias! A world, walking among men,—the world *per se* as a walking man!

And now the musician's eye was lighted up from within. He cast his glance upon phenomena that answered in wondrous reflex, illuminated by his inner light. The essential nature of things now again speaks to him, and he sees things displayed in the calm light of beauty. Again he understands the forest, the brook, the meadow, the blue sky, the gay throng of men, the pair of lovers, the song of birds, the flight of clouds, the roar of storms, the beatitude of blissfully moving repose. All he perceives and constructs is permeated with that wondrous serenity which music has gained through him. Even the tender plaint inherent in all sounds is subdued to a smile: the world regains the innocence of its childhood. "To-day art thou with me in Paradise." Who does not hear the Redeemer's word when listening to the Pastoral Symphony?

The power of shaping the incomprehensible, the never seen, the never experienced, in such wise that it becomes immediately intelligible, now grows apace. The delight in exercising this power becomes humour; all the pain of existence is shattered against the immense delight of playing with it; Brahma, the creator of worlds, laughs as he perceives the illusion about himself; innocence regained plays lightly with the sting of expiated guilt, conscience set free banters itself with the torments it has undergone.

Never has an art offered the world anything so serene as these symphonies in A and F major, and all those works so intimately related to them which the master produced during the divine period of his total deafness. Their effect upon the hearer is that of setting him free from the sense of guilt, just as their after-effect is a feeling of "paradise lost," with which one again turns towards the world of phenomena. Thus these wonderful works preach repentance and atonement in the deepest sense of a divine revelation.

Richard Wagner
Beethoven
1870

Landmark Works

Beethoven's image often crystallizes around a particular piece or small group of works —the symphonies, the string quartets, the piano sonatas— or around the "late Beethoven," that is, the Beethoven of the Missa Solemnis, *the Ninth Symphony, the last string quartets, the last piano sonatas, the* Bagatelles, *and the* Diabelli Variations. *In such an approach, all the other works then seem to revolve around the chosen point of reference—even works not written by Beethoven. Thus the composer himself becomes an anchorage point in the shifting seas of music history.*

The Fifth Symphony

The immeasurably magnificent and profound Symphony in C minor... irresistibly draws the listener in an ever-rising climax into the spirit-realm of the infinite. Nothing could be simpler than the main idea of the opening Allegro, consisting of only two bars and initially in unison, so that the listener is not even certain of the key. The mood of anxious, restless yearning created by this subject is heightened even further by the melodious secondary theme. The breast, constricted and affrighted by presentiments of enormity and annihilation, seems to be struggling for air with a series of stabbing chords, when suddenly a friendly figure moves forward and shines brilliantly through the dreadful darkness of night (the attractive theme in G major that was first touched on by the horns in E flat major). How simple—let it be said once more—is the theme on which the composer has based his entire movement, but how wonderfully all the secondary elements and transition passages are related to it by their rhythmic content, so that they serve to reveal more and more facets of the Allegro's character which the main theme by itself only hints at! All the phrases are short, almost all of them consisting merely of two or three bars, and are also constantly exchanged between winds and strings. One

would think that such ingredients could result only in something disjointed and impossible to follow, but on the contrary it is precisely this overall pattern, and the constant repetition of phrases and single chords, which intensifies to the highest possible degree the feeling of ineffable yearning. Quite apart from the fact that the contrapuntal treatment betokens profound study of the art, the transition passages and constant allusions to the main theme demonstrate how the whole movement with all its impassioned features was conceived in the imagination and clearly thought through.

Does not the lovely theme of the Andante con moto in A flat major sound like the voice of a propitious spirit that fills our breast with hope and comfort? But even here the awful phantom that seized our hearts in the Allegro threatens at every moment to emerge from the storm-cloud into which it disappeared, so that the comforting figures around us rapidly flee from its lightning-flashes. What am I to say about the minuet? Listen to the distinctive modulations, the closes on the dominant major, which is taken up by the bass as the tonic of the following theme in the minor mode, the theme itself, repeatedly extended by a few bars at a time! Does that restless, ineffable yearning, that presentiment of a magical spirit-world, in which the composer excels, not seize hold of you again? But like a shaft of blinding sunlight the full orchestra bursts forth in joyful jubilation with the splendid theme of the final movement. What wonderful contrapuntal intricacies are woven into the overall texture again here! It may well all sweep past many like an inspired rhapsody, but the heart of every sensitive listener is certain to be deeply stirred by one emotion, that of nameless, haunted yearning, and right to the very last chord, indeed for some moments after it, he will be unable to emerge from the magical spirit-realm where he has been surrounded by pain and pleasure in the form of sounds.

The internal disposition of the movements, their working-out, orchestration, the way in which they succeed each other, all is directed towards a single point. But it is particularly the close relationship of the themes to each other which provides the unity that alone is able to sustain *one* feeling in the listener. This relationship frequently becomes clear to the listener when he hears it in the similarity between two passages, or discovers a bass pattern which is common to two different passages; but often a deeper relationship that is not demonstrable in this way speaks only from the heart to the heart, and it is this kind which exists between the subjects of the two Allegros and the minuet, and which brilliantly proclaims the composer's rational genius.

E. T. A. Hoffmann
Kreisleriana

The *Kreutzer* Sonata

"The dinner was like all dinners—stiff and boring. The music began rather early. How every detail of that evening is impressed on my mind! I remember his picking up his violin, unlocking the case, removing the cover some woman had embroidered for him, taking out the instrument, and tuning up. I remember the air of indifference my wife assumed to hide her bashfulness (a bashfulness caused primarily by her playing) and her sitting down with this false expression on her face. Then began the sounding of middle C, the plucking of strings, the setting up of notes. I remember their exchanging looks, their glancing at the assembled guests, their murmuring something to each other, then beginning. She played the first chord. I remember the grave, strained, fine expression that came to his face, as, listening for his tone, he pressed the strings with cautious fingers in response to

View of the Graben, Vienna, in 1781.

the piano. They had begun."

He stopped and made that strange sound several times in succession. When he tried to speak again he could only utter a choking sound, so he waited. Then:

"They played Beethoven's Kreutzer Sonata. Do you know that first *Presto?* do you?" he shouted. "Ugh! A dreadful thing, that sonata. Especially that movement. And in general, music is a dreadful thing. What is it? I don't understand. Just what is music? What does it do to a person? And why does it do it? They say music has an elevating influence on the soul. Nonsense. A lie. It certainly does have an influence, and a terrible influence (I can only speak for myself), but it is not an influence that elevates the soul. It neither elevates nor abases; it merely excites. How shall I put it? Music causes me to forget myself and my true state; it transports me to another state that is not my own. Under the influence of music I fancy I feel things I really do not feel, understand things I do

not understand, am capable of things I am incapable of. I explain it by the fact that music affects me like a yawn, or laughter: I am not sleepy, yet I yawn when I see another yawn; I find nothing to laugh at, yet I laugh on hearing another laugh.

"Music instantly throws me into the spiritual mood in which the composer found himself while writing it. My soul merges with his and I am taken with him from one mood to another, but why I should go through those moods I cannot say. The composer, on the other hand—let's say the composer of the Kreutzer Sonata, Beethoven— knew why he was in that particular mood. The mood led him to the performing of definite acts, and so this mood had sense for him, but it has no sense for me. Music excites to no purpose. To be sure, if a military march is played, the soldiers march off and therefore the music achieves its end; if a dance is played, I dance, and again the music achieves its end. The same thing is true if a mass is played and I take the sacrament. In other cases it merely excites, without supplying any outlet for this excitement. That is why music wields so terrible, sometimes so frightful, an influence. In China music falls under the jurisdiction of the state. And so it should. Is it permissible that any chance person should hypnotize another (or even many others) and make him do whatever he likes? The worst of it is that often the hypnotist is a person of no moral principles.

"It is a dreadful weapon for chance

individuals to wield. Take this Kreutzer Sonata—the first movement. How dare anyone play this *Presto* in a drawing-room where there are women sitting about in *décolleté?*—to play it, applaud it, and then eat ices and exchange the latest gossip? Such music must be played only in very definite and meaningful circumstances, when very definite and meaningful undertakings, corresponding to the music, are to be embarked upon. Once it is played, the actions inspired by the mood must be carried out. Otherwise the unspent feelings and energies, incompatible with the place and the time, are sure to wreak havoc. On me, at least, this music had a devastating effect. It seemed to reveal to me entirely new feelings and capabilities of which I had been utterly unaware. 'This is how it is,' it seemed to say to me; 'not at all as you are used to thinking and being, but like this.' Just what this new way was I could not say, but the consciousness of the new state brought me joy. I saw all the same people, including her and him, in an entirely new light.

"After the *Presto* they played the delightful if commonplace *Andante* with its vulgar variations and weak ending. At the insistence of the guests they played a few other pieces, an elegy by Ernst, it seems, and something else. They were all very nice, but they did not make one-tenth the impression on me that the first piece did. I heard them against the background of the impression made upon me by the first. I was gay and lighthearted for the rest of the evening. Never before had I seen my wife as she was then. The shine of her eyes, the graveness and significance of her expression as she played, and her utter limpness and her faint smile, blissful yet pathetic, when she finished. I saw all that, but the only meaning I attached to it was that she had had revealed to her, just as I had, new and unfamiliar emotions, evoked, as it were, from out the depths of memory.

"The evening ended successfully and everybody went home.

"Knowing that in two days' time I was leaving for the convention, Trukhachevsky said on leaving that he hoped the pleasure he had enjoyed that evening would be repeated the next time he came to our town. I took this to mean that he considered it impossible to visit at my house while I was away, and this pleased me. Since I would not return from the convention before he had left town, I supposed I would not see him again.

"For the first time I shook his hand with genuine pleasure and thanked him for the pleasure. He took leave of my wife, too, as if for a long time. It seemed to me there was nothing in their manner but what was most natural and decorous. Everything was capital. My wife and I were both highly pleased with the evening."

Lev Tolstoy, "The Kreutzer Sonata"

The "Late Beethoven"

The works for which I openly confess my admiration and predilection are for the most part amongst those which conductors more or less renowned . . . have honoured but little, or not at all, with their personal sympathies, so much so that it has rarely happened that they have performed them. These works, reckoning from those which are commonly described nowadays as belonging to Beethoven's *last style* (and which were, not long ago, with lack of reverence, explained by Beethoven's deafness and mental derangement!)— these works, to my thinking, exact from executants and orchestras a *progress* which is being accomplished at this moment—but which is far from being realised in all places—in accentuation, in rhythm, in the manner of phrasing and declaiming certain passages, and of distributing light and shade—in a word, *progress* in the style of the execution itself. They establish, between the musicians of the desks and the *musician chief* who directs them, a link of a nature other than that which is cemented by an imperturbable beating of the time. In many cases even the rough, literal maintenance of the time and of each continuous bar |1, 2, 3, 4, | 1, 2, 3, 4,| clashes with the sense and expression. There, as elsewhere, *the letter killeth the spirit....*

Franz Liszt, Letter to Richard Pohl
5 November 1853

The *Diabelli* Variations

Beethoven didn't stop at the eighteenth century. In the *Song of Gratitude to the Divine Spirit from a Convalescent, in the Lydian Mode* of the 15th string quartet, he pushes himself back to an earlier music, using a polyphony reminiscent of the sixteenth century, and it is likewise to the sixteenth century that the slow "lunar" march (the 20th variation) leads us, first, because of the absence of repeats, and the very slow canon that opens it, mirroring its closing, and also because of the numerous repeated long notes that make one think of the sustained notes on the organ. What exactly did Beethoven know of the music of the sixteenth century? Palestrina, no doubt, a little, but the abundance of chromaticism brings to mind other musicians: Gesualdo, of whom he was most certainly unaware, and de Lassus, who was probably little more to him than a name.

But there is another name that comes to mind when one listens to this movement of shadow and reflections, that of Claude Debussy, notably in the repeated measures that make up the third phrase, a musician who has also relied on an exploration of the past in order to successfully inherit his present.

I have already mentioned Webern, and one of the most fascinating aspects of the *Diabelli Variations* is all the stylistic anticipations they contain. I spoke of Handel regarding the "pathétique" fantasy (31st variation), but I well know that there is another name that comes inevitably to the mind of the modern listener, that of Chopin; all the same, it would not prevent a discussion of Schumann or Mussorgsky in relation to the "dream" prelude (30th variation).

In certain variations the reference to the past is clearest when the premonition of the future is strongest: the slow "lunar" march is at the same time de Lassus and Debussy, the "pathétique," Handel and Chopin. Beethoven, in his exploration of the past, discovered all that was pregnant with the future. Just so, the revolutionaries of France and the United States saw themselves as Greeks and Romans.

Michel Butor
A Dialogue with the Thirty-Three Variations by Ludwig van Beethoven on a Waltz by Diabelli, 1971

An Unknown Symphony

Of all the works of this grandiose composer, this 10th Symphony, which nobody knows, is one of the most sumptuous. Its proportions are on a palatial scale; its ideas are fresh and plentiful; the developments are exact and appropriate.

This Symphony had to exist: the number 9 just wouldn't suit Beethoven. He liked the decimal system: 'I have ten fingers,' he used to explain.

Certain admirers who came dutifully to take in this masterpiece with thoughtful and attentive ears, quite wrongly felt it to be one of Beethoven's inferior works and went so far as to say so. They even went further than that.

In no way can Beethoven be inferior to himself. His form and technique are always portentous, even in his slightest works. In his case the word rudimentary cannot be used. As an artist he can easily stand up to any counterfeit attributed to him.

Erik Satie
Memoirs of an Amnesiac, 1912

The Late String Quartets

There are five. As unalike in their form, color, and intent as are the five fingers of the hand, yet intimately related, the late quartets no longer display kinship with previous works in the same genre; they even seem unrelated to other compositions of the last years. In these works, Beethoven transcended his being to encompass all of humanity.

The Multiple Voices of the Same Soul

This multiple soul, whose inner tragedy was hidden from those who surrounded him, needed, in order to find relief—from the abrupt waves of feelings, from his fits of temper, from his wounded hopes, from his rebellions, his melancholy, and his will to power and to joy despite everything—needed the most supple and intimate polyphony. There was no instrument more responsive to the least inflexions of his thought process than the *string quartet*, with its admirable mobility, its range of four or five octaves, the "dignified equality" of its four melodic parts, for whom a concert is really a debate between the multiple voices of the same soul, between the different people that each person carries inside. Much better than the orchestra, which Beethoven made use of as well during this period—and gladly so, with its magnificent palette of colors—the string quartet maintains and confirms, through its unity of tone, albeit differentiated, the unity of the multiple soul. It would yield marvelously to the analysis of his desires, his contradictory impulses, his discussions with himself, his slow and confused inner process, his battles. Not that the young Beethoven was ready yet to undertake this compelling investigation:

he was caught up between 1800 and 1812, in the whirlwind of the great discourses on the Forum, the triumphal Symphonies. But he began to realize, at a certain moment, to what vehicle he could with greatest confidence entrust his secrets—concurrently so, for a fairly long time, with his long-time interpretative instrument, his trusty steed, his keyboard. But this latter tied him to shows of virtuosity, toward which, at that time, he still found himself attracted, a spur, even, for his genius; in the long term, he was to leave it behind, to the degree that his deafness obliged him to distance himself from the "jousting field," the concert hall, to shut himself in the enclosed world of his soul-universe. Up to the moment where, after his last sonatas, he would refuse to do any more, finding the piano inadequate....

The string quartet was in harmony with his essential needs—also with his deficiencies.

For him, it was a marvelous instrument of intellectual and analytic discrimination, the most supple, precise, sinewy in the entire arsenal of music. Four related instruments, of the same race, and yet each with well-entrenched individualities, capable of asserting the most extreme freedom in the disposition of each voice, yet without shattering the unity of the group sonority—the *Klangeinheit*. Polyphony is, so to speak, natural to them, and it accommodates the debates of the soul with itself, without the risk that one might become too distracted by the sorcery of the polychromy of timbres too different (and, in the orchestral palette, it is other instruments, the woodwinds, the horns, that are the most seductive). Obviously, from the point of view of sensual pleasure, there is an impoverishment: what magical charm does the clarinet not possess in a Mozart quintet! But what is lost in voluptuousness is a gain for the intellect; and the intelligence of the aging Beethoven, whose ear had no doubt remained sensitive to the pleasures of musical colorations…but at the same time dulled to the direct impression of sonorities, would have had less trouble in sacrificing the aural gourmandise to the joy afforded by the pure and severe lines of the quartet. As has been said, the string quartet is a drawing made with two or three pencils, black lead, chalk, red and India ink. And it is well known that drawings by masters are worthy of the most beautiful paintings: it is not out of the question, even, to prefer them, when from the hand of Rembrandt or Leonardo da Vinci. In the tonal drawing of the quartet no subterfuge can be hidden within the austerity of its lines: the dappled veil of *Maya*—that is, the orchestral illusion—cannot be stretched out here to conceal the state of nothingness; "*dice cose…*" (one must have *things* to say and not just empty *words*). Beethoven never spoke when he had nothing to say.

We cannot doubt, on the other hand, that there is not also, in the string quartet, with its bow friction, its vibrations, the extreme acuteness of certain resonances—a nervous action of which nothing (the soft roundness of the woodwinds, their velvetiness, or

the sumptuous material and the golden warmth of the brass instruments)—nothing can mitigate the tense, slightly feverish, at times bony and twisting effect.…But this continuous tension was allied with Beethoven's own; he did not, in his pursuit of expressive means, suppress the sharp gnawings of certain bow strokes. Does that mean that the interpretation ought to pitilessly underscore these, to ally itself purely with the work's intellectual nature? I believe not, because Beethoven was too

great an artist to sacrifice knowingly the beauty of sound to its meaning. His wholesome ear would have married one to the other.

Romain Rolland
La Cathédrale Interrompue

A Player of the Late Quartets

I have felt for a long time that for a listener to get inside these late string quartets, he must try to delve into Beethoven's innermost thoughts. We can take for granted the fantastic craftsmanship, the intellect of a great mind, for these exist also in his other works. What Beethoven has to say about life in his music cannot be described in words. However there are many words and indications that he himself wrote in the score to help the performers realize his feelings and, if we can understand these markings, then we are nearer to getting into Beethoven's mind. I am not talking about tempo indications, which are valuable in themselves, but all the extra instructions, some of which are very unusual and seem spontaneous. Reading them with the music, one can almost feel

Beethoven actually writing this music....

The number of markings, dynamic changes, extra instructions, make a tremendous impression on the performer. Beethoven adds another dimension to the music. It is almost as though he is adding hand gestures while talking to you. The reason for all the markings becomes obvious though, when you realize that a lot of them, at least in my opinion, are against the natural phrasing. There are numerous examples of sudden changes from forte to piano and vice versa. This is to create and designate an extra tension. Neither does Beethoven economise in his use of dynamics. For example in the Op. 130 *Andante con moto ma non troppo*, underneath which he wrote *poco scherzoso* (a little jokingly), in some bars there is a change of dynamic on almost every note. Two bars have five changes!

Peter Cropper, First Violin
Lindsay String Quartet
Beethoven: The Late Quartets Nos. 12–16
4-record set, 1983

The Tearing Asunder

He no longer connects to the image the landscape, now abandoned and alienated. He sweeps it with the same fire that inflames subjectivity, while this, in its flight, hits up against the structural partitions of the work, faithful to the idea of its dynamic. His late works remain a process: not, however, in the sense of development, but as an "ignition" between two extremes that no longer tolerate the middle ground or harmony, the act of spontaneity. Between these two extremes, in the most technical sense of the word: here, homophony, unison, the flower of significant rhetoric; and there, the polyphony that immediately rises to the beyond.

It falls to subjectivity to encompass these two extremes in a single moment, that fills the polyphonic texture with its tensions, the breeze in harmony, and that escapes from it, leaving behind the denuded sound, which implants the flower of rhetoric like a commemorative

monument to the past, into which enters subjectivity itself, petrified. The caesuras, however, the sudden stop, that signal the late Beethoven more than anything else, are moments of eruptions; the work falls silent when it is thus forsaken, and transfers its "voids" to the exterior.

Only then does the following fragment join on, captivated on the spot by subjectivity's order, escaping and complicit, all risk assumed from the preceding fragment. For the secret is between them and does not let itself be evoked other than through the figure they form together. This illuminates the countersense, according to which the late Beethoven is described as subjective and objective. Objective is the fragile landscape, subjective is the light by means of which this landscape blazes. Beethoven does not bring about their harmonic synthesis. He tears them asunder in time, as a power of dissociation, perhaps in order to perpetuate them for eternity.

In the history of art, late works are catastrophes.

Theodor W. Adorno, 1937
in *L'Arc*, no. 40, 1990

The Ninth Symphony

The boundless Ninth Symphony challenges the symphonic form to the breaking point—for the first time, linking orchestra with voice, solo and choral. It is to the future of music what the big bang is to the history of the universe. Both mesmerize. It is the fusion of desire and idea.

K. K. Hoftea

Große m

Herrn

Deliverance Through Joy

In the Ninth Symphony, Beethoven created his most masterful structure. His conception reveals its staggering grandeur from the very first, in the way he arrives at the opening theme—the fifth step of the scale, the first step, then lower to the subdominant and so on, like open triads. These notes begin the struggle of life and death, and for the first two movements Beethoven is engaged in mortal combat. When I conduct the second movement, I cannot escape the sensation that death itself is staring over my shoulder. Even the Presto brings no relief; for all its sweetness it is only a spectre that flickers briefly across the scene. In the third movement Beethoven approaches his end. Death knocks at the door with trumpets, and Beethoven refuses, in the violins. His answer is "no" until the very last movement. But at the close of this movement he meets his inevitable death. For decades I have felt it in just this way. For me the finale simply does not take place here on earth. It

nächst dem Kärnthnerthore.

...sikalische Akademie

von

van Beethoven,

is dangerous to talk so specifically about one's personal vision, but in my mind's eye I see quite clearly the instant in which Beethoven enters Heaven. The finale tells me of his arrival, and how all of Heaven stands still at his presence. Significantly enough, Beethoven no longer found sufficient means within the orchestra to tell us all he wanted to say in his music. He returned, instead, to the fountainhead of all instruments, to the human voice—the voice of man, whom God created in his own image. Beethoven prepared us for the entry of this voice in the course of an elaborate and symbolic transition. The recitative for contrabasses in the finale's introduction is constantly interrupted by themes from earlier movements. What does he mean by these interruptions? They are explained by the soloist's first words: "Oh, friends, not these tones…" In effect: away with the conflict, away with the memory of pain and of death— "Let us raise our voices in more pleasing and more joyful sounds!" Each time I conduct this music I experience it anew as something that is ineffably com-

plete in itself. In the other symphonies, Beethoven speaks of redemption through freedom, through nature, through the conquest of fate, through divine gaiety and the boundless energies of the dance, but here the theme is man's deliverance through joy.

Josef Krips
The Symphonies of Beethoven
London Symphony Orchestra
8-record set, 1963

So Much the Worse for the Law!

In the adagio cantabile the principle of unity is so little observed that it might rather be regarded as two distinct pieces than as one. The first melody, in B flat and in common time, is succeeded by another melody, absolutely different from it, in triple time, and in D. Then the first theme, slightly altered and varied by the first violins, makes a second appearance in the original key, for the purpose of reintroducing the triple melody. This now appears without either alteration or variation in the key of G; after which the first theme definitively installs itself, and does not again

On 22 May 1872 the Ninth Symphony was performed at Bayreuth under Wagner's baton.

permit its rival subject to share with it the attention of the listener.

Several hearings are necessary before one can altogether become accustomed to so singular a disposition of this marvellous adagio. As to the beauty of all these melodies, the infinite grace of the ornaments applied to them, the sentiments of melancholy tenderness, of passionate sadness, and of religious meditation which they express, if my prose could give of all this even an approximate idea, music would have found in the "written word" such a competitor as even the greatest of all poets was never able to oppose to it. It is an immense work; and, when once its powerful charm has been experienced, the only answer for the critic who reproaches the composer for having violated the law of unity is: *So much the worse for the law!*

We are now approaching the moment when the vocal and orchestral elements are to be united. The violoncellos and double basses intone the recitative, of which we have already spoken, after a ritornello of the wind instruments as violent and rough as a cry of anger....

This symphony is the most difficult of all by this composer; its performance necessitating study, both patient and repeated; but, above all, well directed. It requires, moreover, a number of singers greater than would otherwise be necessary; as the chorus is evidently supposed to cover the orchestra in many places; and, also, because the manner in which the music is set to the words and the excessive height of some of the vocal parts render voice production difficult, and diminish the volume and energy of the sounds produced.

Hector Berlioz
A Critical Study of Beethoven's Nine Symphonies, 1862

Ode to Joy

O friends, no more these sounds!
Let us sing more cheerful songs,
more full of joy!

Joy, bright spark of divinity,
Daughter of Elysium,
Fire-inspired we tread
Thy sanctuary.
Thy magic power re-unites
All that custom has divided,
All men become brothers
Under the sway of thy gentle wings.

Whoever has created
An abiding friendship,
Or has won
A true and loving wife,
All who can call at least one soul theirs,
Join in our song of praise;
But any who cannot must creep
tearfully
Away from our circle.

All creatures drink of joy
At nature's breast.
Just and unjust
Alike taste of her gift;
She gave us kisses and the fruit of the
vine,
A tried friend to the end.
Even the worm can feel contentment,
And the cherub stands before God!

Gladly, like the heavenly bodies
Which He set on their courses
Through the splendor of the
firmament;

Thus, brothers, you should run your
race,
As a hero going to conquest.

You millions, I embrace you.
This kiss is for all the world!
Brothers, above the starry canopy
There must dwell a loving Father.
Do you fall in worship, you millions?
World, do you know your Creator?
Seek Him in the heavens!
Above the stars must He dwell.

Friedrich Schiller,
"Ode to Joy"

Thoughts of a Ghost

In the Ninth Symphony, that most intimate, most profound mirror of Beethoven's thinking, one finds mixed together a burning mysticism, an intuitionism passionate about God in

Nature and in the moral conscience, a Germano-mythic theosophism nourished on Schiller, on philosophical readings, perhaps on Schelling, on his links with Eastern thinkers—all of it blended with a will to act heroically and revolutionarily, in the spirit of the Zeitgeist of his youth. Because, at the time when he had this symphony played, he was already a "ghost": the Vienna of 1825 was already far from the Bonn of 1792. And it is to the latter that Beethoven's ideas remained faithful: he maintained the dreams of his youth, those of the Schillers and the Kants, even while living in the age of the disenchanted Romantics and the Epicurean skeptics, of Byron and Rossini (to name but two of the greatest). He was a stranger among these new generations, a man from another century—a man standing above all centuries. Likewise, he was never understood, even by his friends. He inspired a respect in the best of them, in which could be sensed something of the religious—as if it were directed toward an inspired soul from another age.

A curious thing is that he is closer to our time—probably without being any better understood. The instinct of the masses sense dimly in him, in his *Ninth*, not so much the past but the future, of which he seems an almost mythic harbinger. Because if his *Ninth* is, in fact, the culmination of a great epoch of humanity, the completion of the aspirations of its mind and its heart —and if this epoch has passed—it has left survivors, in the iron age that we traverse at present (1941), as well as an abandoned temple in the middle of the deserts, the imperishable documentation of the great Dream—always a sanctuary for men's hearts—of the kingdom of God on Earth, established by the brotherhood of men, in reason and in joy.

Whatever it is, it is striking that the common people have, even more than the elite, always reserved a place apart for the *Ninth Symphony* among all musical works—in spite of the purists, who are offended that this homage is directed to something beyond music.

We do not share this reservation: because we know that music loses nothing by it. Because music is full of thought does not mean that we make it subordinate to thought! They mutually enrich each other, without one or the other being sacrificed. And it is not the least of this symphony's triumphs that the two can realize their relationship within it. For centuries, in the course of centuries, people have debated, and they will continue to debate, this difficult question of the relationship of poetry and music brought together. It has been cut off, too peremptorily, by some in favor of the absolute supremacy of music, by others "in favor of the Muses over the Sirens," as might have been said in the eighteenth century. Beethoven has resolved it (particularly in the *finale* of this symphony) by the perfect fountain of thought with music. Let us note: he did not obtain it through a scrupulous attention to the words....he treated freely—let us say, rather, largely—Schiller's text. But by so doing, he recreated the spirit and the substance; he made them his own; he transfused them with the blood of his music.

Romain Rolland
La Cathédrale Interrompue, 1966

Performance of the Ninth Symphony,
7 May 1824

Beethoven on Film

Over the years many filmmakers have turned their attention to Beethoven. Most of them have reconstituted the "Beethoven myth," with its host of clichés about the rebel, the uncompromising genius, the tragic hero. In 1936, with Un grand amour de Beethoven *(Beethoven's Great Love), Abel Gance became the first to use a soundtrack. It may prove unsettling to see Beethoven sit down at the piano as the sound of an entire orchestra pours forth from the instrument.*

"Un grand amour de Beethoven"

Scenario to Abel Gance's movie, illustrated on the following pages

This "great love" was the one Beethoven harbored for Giulietta Guicciardi, whom he met in the salons of Vienna in 1801; however, she felt only great friendship and admiration for him in return. One summer night, as Beethoven improvised the piece that would be christened the *Moonlight* Sonata, Giulietta confessed to him that she was about to marry the young, handsome Count Gallenberg. Deeply wounded, Beethoven fled into the storm raging outside. Little by little, he became aware that he was deaf. He sought sanctuary in the old Heiligenstadt windmill. Some time later, Beethoven returned to Vienna and shut himself off. The one person to whom he opened his door was the sweet, loving Therese von Brunsvik, Giulietta's cousin. An old friend, she had guessed the story behind his broken heart. At Giulietta's wedding, Beethoven angrily pounded out a funeral march on the organ, greatly upsetting the ceremony. Gallenberg, however, soon proved to be a gambler and a cad. Giulietta understood, but too late, Beethoven's despair. He sought to ease his pain through Therese; gradually they drew close. But Giulietta, unhappy, wanted to confess her error to Beethoven and be forgiven. His deafness necessitated that she write down her feelings. Overcome, the composer began the famed letter to the "Immortal Beloved." Therese, who dropped by, found it and thought it was meant for her; Beethoven dared not tell her the truth. In lying, he spared her but ruined his own hopes for happiness.

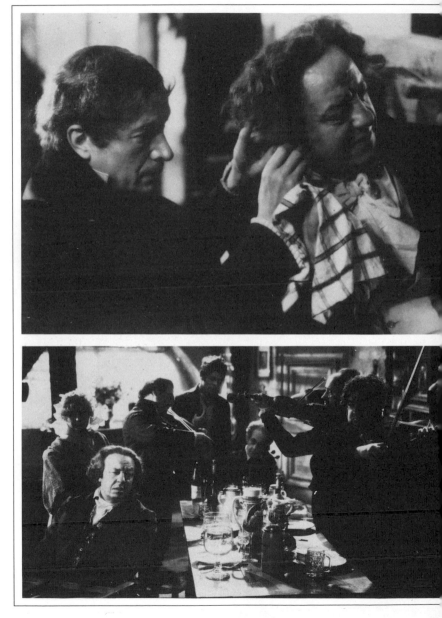

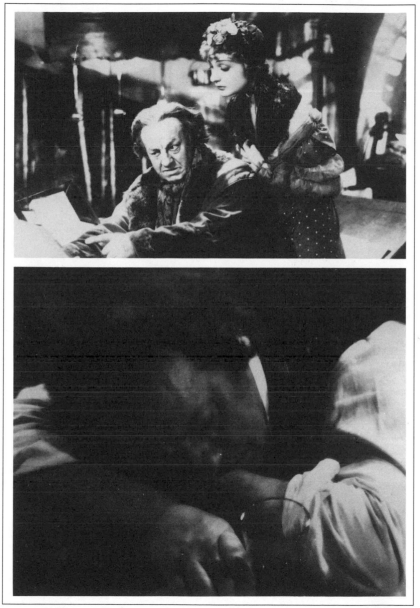

List of Illustrations

Further Reading

Musical Works

Two monumental publications cover the ensemble of Beethoven's compositions: *Beethovens Werke*, 25 volumes, published by Breitkopf & Härtel; and *Werke*, edited by Joseph Schmidt-Görg, in course of publication since 1961 by the Beethoven-Haus in Bonn. Kinsky and Halm's *Das Werk Beethovens* (Munich and Duisberg, 1955) is the standard catalogue of Beethoven's work.

Principal Works in English

Cooper, Barry, editor, *The Beethoven Compendium* (London, 1991)

Scherman, Thomas K., and Biancolli, Louis, editors, *The Beethoven Companion* (New York, 1972)

Schindler, Anton, *Beethoven as I Knew Him* (Münster, 1860), translated by Constance S. Jolly (London, 1966, reprinted 1972)

Solomon, Maynard, *Beethoven* (New York, 1977)

Thayer, Alexander W. *The Life of Ludwig van Beethoven* (Berlin, 1866), 2 volumes, edited by Elliot Forbes (Princeton, N.J., 1964, 1967)

Tovey, Donald, *Beethoven*, edited by Hubert J. Foss (London, 1944, reprinted 1975)

Letters and Conversation Books

The Letters of Beethoven, collected, translated, and edited by Emily Anderson (London, 1961)

Letters, Journals and Conversations, edited by Michael Hamburger (London, 1951, reprinted 1984)

Discography

Since its beginnings, the phonograph record has put itself at Beethoven's disposition. Rare are the artists who have not at one time attempted to show what they could do with the *Moonlight* Sonata or the Fifth Symphony. But many interpreters of great talent have also been inclined toward works that are lesser known without being less interesting, with the result that no work of Beethoven worthy of attention has been overlooked by the recording medium. Even on the compact disc (CD) format, this repertoire enjoys exceptional representation. The only important gap is that of some of the vocal works, which are less well represented on long-playing records as well. Today, a complete Beethovian discography can be made with CDs alone, which was done here.

This richness of choice (especially for the sonatas, string quartets, and symphonies), added to a fifty-disc limit in representing the "essential Beethoven," has led to the following guidelines: only one interpretation of each work has been proposed; complete sets were favored; and any CD not entirely devoted to Beethoven (which eliminates, for example, any recording of the Quintet for Piano and Winds, op. 16) was rejected. Finally, the selection was geared toward current interpretive tendencies —without, however, omitting those historic recordings (for example, those of Wilhelm Backhaus, David Oistrakh, Josef Krips) that, to one degree or another, are models for any modern reading of Beethoven.

Solo Piano

Sonatas, Alfred Brendel (11 discs, Philips)
Diabelli Variations, Grigory Sokolov (1, ABC, includes the Piano Sonata op. 111)
Bagatelles, Daniel Blumenthal (1, Calliope)

Chamber Music

Sonatas for Violin and Piano, David Oistrakh, Lev Oborine (4, Philips)
Sonatas for Cello and Piano, Vladimir Rostropovich, Sviatoslav Richter (2, Philips)
Trios for Piano, Violin, and Cello, Vladimir Ashkenazy, Itzhak Perlman, Lynn Harrell (4, EMI)
String Quartets, Alban Berg Quartet (10, EMI, in 3 vols)
Septet for Violin, Viola, Cello, Contrabass, Clarinet, French Horn, and Bassoon, members of the New Octet of Vienna (1, Decca, includes the *Trio*, op. 11)

Orchestral Music

Concerto for Violin and Orchestra, Itzhak Perlman, Philharmonia Orchestra, cond. Carlo Maria Giulini (1, EMI)
Concertos for Piano and Orchestra, Wilhelm Backhaus, Vienna Philharmonic, cond. Hans Schmidt-Isserstedt (3, Decca)
Concerto for Piano, Violin, Cello, and Orchestra, Mark Zeltser, Anne-Sophie Mutter, Yo Yo

Ma, Berlin Philharmonic, cond. Herbert von Karajan (1, Deutsche Grammophon) *Symphonies*, London Philharmonic Orchestra, with, for the Ninth Symphony, soloists Jennifer Vyvyan, Shirley Carter, Rudolf Petrak,

Donald Bell, and the BBC Choir, cond. Josef Krips (6, Sonia Classic, distr. Schott)

Vocal Works

Fidelio, Hildegard Behrens, Peter Adtmann, Hans Sotin, Theo Adam,

Chicago Symphony and Choir, cond. Georg Solti (2, Decca) *The Mount of Olives*, Monica Pick-Hieronimi, James Anderson, Victor von Halem, Choeurs et Orchestre National de Lyon, cond. Serge Baudo (1, Harmonia

Mundi) *Missa Solemnis*, Lella Cuberli, Trudeliese Schmidt, Vinson Cole, José Van Dam, Vienna Singverein, Berlin Philharmonic, cond. Herbert von Karajan (2, Deutsche Grammophon)

Index